THE POWER
OF PASSIONATE
INTENTION

THE POWER
OF PASSIONATE
INTENTION

The Elisha Principle

MARK CHIRONNA

DESTINY IMAGE® PUBLISHERS, INC.

P.O. Box 310, Shippensburg, PA 17257-0310

"Speaking to the Purposes of God for This Generation and for the Generations to Come."

This book and all other Destiny Image, Revival Press, MercyPlace, Fresh Bread, Destiny Image Fiction, and Treasure House books are available at Christian bookstores and distributors worldwide.

For a U.S. bookstore nearest you, call 1-800-722-6774.

For more information on foreign distributors, call 717-532-3040.

Reach us on the Internet: www.destinyimage.com.

ISBN 10: 0-7684-3156-5   ISBN 13: 978-0-7684-3156-8

For Worldwide Distribution, Printed in the U.S.A.

1 2 3 4 5 6 7 8 9 10 11 / 13 12 11 10

Previously published as *The Elisha Principle: Jordan Revisited*
by Destiny Image Publishers, 1989.

ISBN 1-56043-006-0   ISBN 978-1-5604-3006-3

ENDORSEMENTS

The prophetic is a tough business. You are either right or wrong and there is no hiding place. There are numerous critics and seasonal friends. I have always admired Mark's work, though we have not met. He has prevailed in a hard business and much of that is down to passion and intentionality.

We are living in times that require the presence of the modern day equivalent of David's Mighty Men. We need champions and warriors—people with a passionate love for Jesus and a hatred of the devil and all his works.

Jesus went about doing good and healing all who were oppressed of the devil. We need to see a people who are not earthbound in their spirituality but who know how to rise up and police the heavens—dynamic men and women who can live from heaven to earth.

The Power of Passionate Intention contains the power of a life message that I will be using with my disciples. Thanks Mark.

Graham Cooke
Founder, Brilliant Book House
Author, *A Divine Confrontation*

The Church is changing, and while it is sometimes painful, God's people must not be stalled by change. In *The Power of Passionate Intention,* Dr. Chironna so simply explores how the Church must be prepared for God's next move toward building His kingdom. Of course, there is a time to honor tradition, but there is also a time to make a clean break from the status quo. As you read this book, based on the powerful "Elisha Principle," you will learn how to have your foot on the starter block, ready to move with excitement for the Lord. Make this book part of your spiritual library and discover how God provides for the changes He mandates—and how He will bless your dreams when you are in relationship with Him.

Bishop Eddie L. Long
Senior Pastor, New Birth Missionary Baptist Church

To all who are hungry for more of God, Mark Chironna tells us how to move to the next level in The Elisha Principle. Using the process of the passing of the mantle from Elijah to Elisha, this book is a wonderfully wise "how to" for believers who want to serve on the front lines of God's end time army. I've known Mark for over 20 years. There are few men as well equipped to see in the invisible realm and impart to us powerful eternal truths. For me this book is a life-changing instant classic.

Dr. Mahesh Chavda
Senior Pastor, All Nations Church

Here we go...Mark has done it again! Dr. Mark is a living reservoir of revelation and every sentence he writes is like a paragraph of wisdom. *The Power of Passionate Intention* is a landmark achievement and a very timely book in these days of uncertainty and fear. I encourage everyone to get this book and experience another dose of extraordinary inspiration from the pen of Mark Chironna.

Dr. Myles Munroe
Consultant and Leadership Coach
Author, *Rediscovering the Kingdom*
BFM International, Nassau Bahamas

As the Church, sometimes we are relevant only to ourselves and not to the world we live in. To be effective in this new millennium we can no longer operate in a 1950's mindset and style. With brilliant insight into the Word, once again Dr. Mark Chironna leads us to a wellspring of truth where we can drink deep and come away invigorated and renewed to serve our generation with fresh relevance!

Gary Oliver
Pastor, Tabernacle of Praise
President of Gary Oliver Enterprises

We are truly on the precipice of God doing some new things on the earth. *The Power of Passionate Intention* is a timely message that should not be missed. The importance of preparing for a generational transfer cannot be understated.

Mark Chironna does a masterful job of helping us see what the real issues are and how to fulfill our destiny of changing God's reputation and revealing His glory in the earth.

Bob Mumford
Founder, Life Changers
Author, *Agape Road*

Mark Chirona's *The Power of Passionate Intention* is profound, insightful, and spiritually explosive if applied to your life. It will change the way you view everything. It may also change the way everyone views you.

Mark reveals how true spirituality is more than just existing as a Christian, it is filled with forethought and divinely given intention and it will change the world.

John Paul Jackson
Founder, Streams Ministries International
Author, *Unmasking the Jezebel Spirit
and Needless Casualties of War*

Dr. Mark Chironna has really put together a thoughtful and practical but profound book in his *The Power of Passionate Intention*. I love how Dr. Mark balances his perspective on where we are in the Christian world with the need to position our lives and be deliberate in our pursuit of God. I felt like a theologian just life coached me! What a blend!

Shawn Bolz
Author of *Keys to Heaven's Economy*
and *The Throne Room Company*
Senior Pastor of Expression58

In the Book of Beginnings, Genesis, the first mention of the Holy Spirit is that *He moved...* Do you think that might give us a clue concerning the very nature of God Himself? He moved in the beginning; He has moved in sequential waves of emphasis in past church history; and He surely moves today! That encourages me. That means He will surely help motivate and move upon us as individual believers and as the corporate Body of Christ into His divine purposes for our generation and beyond.

Mark Chironna unveils revelation on these truths through the life example of Elisha in the living classic that you hold in your hand. It is with joy and honor that I commend to you *The Power of Passionate Intention.* May the power of the written word contained herein resonate within your being and create a greater passionate desire for Christ's presence, power and purposes in each of our lives.

James W. Goll
Encounters Network • Prayer Storm • Compassion Acts
Author of *The Seer* and *The Lost Art of Intercession*

Now, more than any other time in church history, God's people stand at the precipice of a monumental shift in the Body of Christ requiring keen spiritual discernment and precise revelatory direction. In the years that I have known Mark Chironna I have found that he possesses the unique qualities of clear spiritual insight with profound intellectual depth that allows him to present deep and complicated Kingdom principles in simple and understandable ways. Clearly, *The Power of Passionate Intention* is the result of that gifting and a much-needed clarion call to the Bride of Christ in preparation for this transition. Both Joshua and Elisha are profound spiritual prototypes to highlight the emergence of many in this generation who will do mighty exploits and bring great glory to God's Kingdom.

The book that you hold in your hand will help lay the foundation for that mandate and establish Biblical parameters that will keep us from the mirky spiritual ditches that lay on either side of the straight and narrow way. I truly recommend this book to any desperate and hungry believer longing to know Jesus more intimately and represent His kingdom with integrity, power and humility.

Paul Keith Davis
Founder, WhiteDove Ministries

In his book, *The Power of Passionate Intention,* Mark Chironna unearths hidden keys from the life of Elijah and Elisha that unlock buried treasure in the Body of Christ. Like a skilled archeologist, Mark uncovers the veiled mysteries etched on the hearts of these men and written on the topography of ancient cities. He takes us on a prophetic journey back to our future as he systematically explains the modern significance of lesson taught centuries ago.

This manuscript is a textbook on the coming reformation and is filled with timeless insights. I recommend this book to anyone who wants to impact their world for Christ.

Kris Vallotton
Co-Founder of the *Bethel School of Supernatural Ministry.*
Author of five books including *The Supernatural Ways of Royalty.*
Senior Associate Leader of Bethel Church,
Redding CA

In his book, *The Power of Passionate Intention,* Dr. Mark Chironna releases a clarion call to seek first the Kingdom of Heaven and to live completely abandoned to the destiny of God over your life. As a man who carries and displays the Father heart of God, Mark reveals dynamic spiritual principles that will break you out of what many would consider "normal Christian living" into a supernatural lifestyle that God has fashioned us for.

If you're hungry for breakthrough, this prophetic message will act as a catalyst to ignite faith and passion in your life so you can better lay hold of that which exists in the realm of *eternity* and bring it into the realm of *now!*

This book is a must read for everyone

Jeff Jansen
Founder of Global Fire Ministries International &
GFM World Miracle Center, Nashville, TN
Author of Glory Rising

Mark Chironna says more on accident than most people say on purpose! His book is clear, insightful, balanced, and biblically sound. It will ignite fresh fire in you!

Bishop Dale C. Bronner
Author/Senior Pastor
Word of Faith Family Worship Cathedral

Prophets and prophecy - has there ever been a greater need for a Biblical, sound, but excited response to the fact that God speaks through special mouthpieces! But history is littered with those who seemed to start so well but finished in disarray, even disgrace. This sensible, scriptural book will help keep prophets and prophecy on course. God has so much to say - He looks for people to speak to and through right now! Mark has done the Body of Christ a great service with this book.

Gerald Coates
Speaker, Author, and Broadcaster
Founder, Pioneer Network

This book's title *The Power of Passionate Intention* says it all. My friend Dr. Mark Chironna has packed all three of those ingredients in this high impact book. You will find power, passion, and intention. Power because of the source of the content—the Bible. Passion because that captures the essence of the author. Intention—now, that is all up to you. I guarantee you that if you go beyond reading this book and bear down with intentionality you will have passionate power. Buckle your seat belt—you are about to take off.

Dr. Samuel R. Chand
Leadership Architect and Change Strategist
Former Pastor, College President, Chancellor
President Emeritus of Beulah Heights Bible College

———————

I've known Mark Chironna for many years now and have watched him morph and mature into one of the leading Prophets of this Generation. The passion he demonstrates in the delivery of the Word is a force to be reckoned with. The Power of Passionate Intention is one of many great pieces of literature Mark has penned. I have been privileged to minister with Mark on many occasions and the "fusion" of our gifts/expressions took us both to new heights in our ministries. Get ready to go to those new heights in your own lives and ministries as you are prophetically challenged and stimulated by this inspiring work. Truly Mark's tongue is that of a ready writer.

Kim Clement
Author, *Call Me Crazy, but I'm Hearing God's Voice:*
Secrets to Hearing the Voice of God

CONTENTS

Foreword 19

Preface 21

Chapter 1: The Elisha Principle 25

Chapter 2: When the Cloud Moves, Move 33

Chapter 3: From Gilgal to Father's House 45

Chapter 4: We Are Standing on Holy Ground 63

Chapter 5: Roll, Jordan, Roll! 75

Chapter 6: Crossing Over on Dry Ground 83

Chapter 7: What Do You Want? 95

Chapter 8: Have a Single Eye 103

Chapter 9: Grief Before Growth 113

Chapter 10: Love Releases…Fear Possesses 125

Chapter 11: The Menace of "Muddy" Waters 131

Chapter 12: The Clear Stream at Antioch 143

Chapter 13: Jordan and Beyond 155

Chapter 14: The Elisha Season 163

FOREWORD

A fresh stirring is arising in the hearts of God's people all over the earth. I've seen it in city after city, nation after nation. Every tribe in God's wonderful Church seems to have felt a longing in their hearts for more. This longing closely resembles birth pangs because something is being birthed that will affect the course of world history. A new generation sees the dawn of a new day. Yet what is happening must not be untended as a river without banks or a host of musicians without a conductor. We are in a divine moment. We must now hear from the prophets. Our passion needs understanding, and our sense of destiny must now merge with divine wisdom.

The re-release of Mark Chironna's *The Elisha Principle* comes at just the right time, giving us the very word we need. He carries such a prophetic perspective—both of the day we live in and the biblical pattern that will take us to the next level. Mark brilliantly draws understanding from the life of Elisha and lays out for the reader a pattern that must be embraced. Elisha's life profoundly parallels the life of the believer who is desperate for increase.

We must correctly steward the dream that has been planted in our hearts. This book teaches us how to maintain the focus and drive to pursue that God-given dream, without being ship-wrecked by discouragement or distractions. The author wisely leads us to turn what would normally derail our faith into a tool that propels us into our destiny, thus preparing individuals to function as members of the body of Christ. We will see the glory of God manifested through us, demonstrating signs and wonders outside the walls of the church, bringing the Kingdom to a world hungry for a pure demonstration of the Gospel.

The Church stands as an Elisha generation, knowing there is more. As Elisha pursued Elijah, the Church today must pursue the mantle of our elder brother, Jesus Christ. This book paints a clear picture of what God has made available through the cross to those who are willing to believe. The Lord offers us not merely salvation from the sentence of hell but an invitation to walk in the increased anointing of the One who has gone before us. The time is now. Embrace the journey, and let's together bring in a harvest that is worthy of the Lamb who was slain.

Bill Johnson
Pastor – Bethel Church
Author – *When Heaven Invades Earth and Face to Face with God*
iBethel.org
BJM.org

PREFACE

Great days are ahead for the Lord's army! Regardless of world events and the challenges faced by God's people, my understanding of Him and of the Scriptures keeps me from developing a doom-and-gloom picture of the future Church.

The Church has wrinkles yet to be ironed out; but, despite her weaknesses, I believe revival, restoration, and victory lay ahead. Many in the Body of Christ would agree; together, we live in expectation of the next wave of the Holy Spirit.

Still, while we look ahead to even greater glory, we must beware not to become so revival-assured and rapture-oriented as to inadvertently resign the world to the forces of antichrist. God *is* building a Church without *"spot or wrinkle"* (Eph. 5:27)—and *we* are involved in preparing her for the Bridegroom, the Lord Jesus Christ!

At every stage in her development, the Lord desires His Church to be a living organism through which He manifests His glory to the world. Too often, what we offer Him instead is a languishing organization (albeit one that He continues patiently to groom and grow).

With each visitation from Heaven, God has drawn His people into a deeper revelation of His Word. His means are always tailored to the people's needs at the time. In Exodus 25:8-9 the Lord promised Moses a detailed, practical plan:

> *Let them construct a sanctuary for Me, that I may dwell among them. According to all that I am going to show you, as the pattern of the tabernacle and the pattern of all its furniture, just so you shall construct it.*

Under Moses' direction, the people proceeded according to God's commands. As a result, *"the cloud covered the tent of meeting, and the glory of the Lord filled the tabernacle"* (Exod. 40:34).

The principle revealed here warrants our consideration. Visitation (the cloud of glory) did not come until all things were done according to the divine pattern. That is the key to restoration in the Body of Christ. In Acts 3:19-21, Peter declared:

> *Therefore repent and return, so that your sins may be wiped away, in order that **times** of refreshing may come from the presence of the Lord; and that He may send Jesus, the Christ appointed for you, whom heaven must receive until the **period of restoration** of all things about which God spoke by the mouth of His holy prophets from ancient time.*

Peter spoke of *times* or *periods* of restoration. If we assume that this passage from Acts speaks only of the days after the Second Coming, we overlook the full weight of the passage. This is not just about restoration in the Millennium or for a future Jewish race. The prophets spoke primarily of spiritual restoration. They foresaw an age during which God's people would exemplify the character of God before the nations. Many Old Testament passages describing the glory of God over Zion find their ultimate fulfillment in the Church. We have come to Zion (see Heb. 12:22).

Since the day of Pentecost, times of restoration and refreshing have come from the presence of the Lord. Every outpouring of the Spirit since that time has fulfilled Peter's sermon and the words of the prophets. This is true of the Charismatic Renewal and all the moves of God that have ebbed and flowed in the days since it began.

God is ever planning a new thing in the earth; therefore, His people should always be expectant of what is to come. The ripened grain awaits harvest…He sends early rains and latter rains to water His fields of wheat…clouds are gathering and a new rain of glory will burst forth.

Are we ready for it? When God moves, do we move with Him? Will the next visitation produce lasting effects upon the Church and the world? Or will we fulfill the old proverb: "He who forgets the past is doomed to repeat it"?

While every move of God including the Charismatic movement has been wonderful and exciting and real, many things have gone awry. Because we tend to elevate our natural desires above God's spiritual ones, we undermine His building process. In the midst of renewal and revival, we often muddy the crystal-clear waters that issue forth from His Throne; we do this with the hand of fleshly indulgence.

I believe a greater wave is coming. As the people of God, we must be prepared and available. This book is written as a word of preparation and admonition to help us learn from past mistakes and *"press on to maturity"* (Heb. 6:1).

May the Lord breathe upon the words of this book by His Spirit according to the very inspiration and insight He has asked me to share with you. May He multiply it as He did the loaves and fishes—and feed multitudes.

Chapter 1

The Elisha Principle

Today's world is in transition. Global shifts are occurring on a broad scale. Fundamental changes are being realized in the arenas of politics, finance, and international relations. We are in an era where it seems no stone is left unturned. Everywhere, the familiar is giving way to the unknown.

As Scripture has shown time and again, what happens in the natural realm is a precursor of what is coming in the supernatural. While the world hurtles through global transition, the Church approaches its own crossroads, a spiritual line of demarcation—the end of one 500-year period and entry into another.

> What happens in the natural realm is a precursor of what is coming in the supernatural.

God has often marked spiritual epochs in 500-year increments that begin with powerful, supernatural moves. I believe this transition will be no exception. What God is bringing to the Body of Christ is a magnificent milestone in His 1,000-year process of restoring to the Church the pure message of the cross and of grace that had been all but lost to the medieval Church prior to the Reformation.

I believe that what is coming will rival what took place during the Great Reformation! Once again, a tidal wave of His glory, a kind of 500-year spiritual flood, a whirlwind that lifts the sails of His people and carries them into new waters will usher in the new. Unlike natural storms that wreak havoc and wreck lives, this storm is not to be feared. Instead, it is a tidal surge in which we are to immerse ourselves with abandon.

What's coming is a season during which one generation will pass from the scene and leave the legacy of the anointing to the generation that follows. It is a pivotal time comparable to the days in which the mantle dropped from Elijah's shoulders as he exited the earth in a chariot of fire. In a great biblical transfer of the anointing, Elisha took up his master's coat and succeeded him. Not only did Elisha inherit the anointing of Elijah—he received a double portion, just as he requested! (See Second Kings 2:9.)

From our twenty-first-century perspective, the Charismatic Renewal (which began in the 1960s and has spawned subsequent renewals and revivals ever since) can be compared to the ministry of Elijah.[1] As we proceed through the various moves of God, I believe the Church is positioned for a season that parallels Elisha's ministry—and what is occurring today will, in its fullness, far surpass all that has gone before!

Hence *The Power of Passionate Intention: The Elisha Principle.*

But what is the principle at the center of this book? Briefly, the Elisha Principle is the profound and powerful tenet that operated in Elisha's life and thrust him onto the front lines of God's army.

That is where we want to be: in the front lines...on the cutting edge...in the thick of

> If we desire to see and be part of a great move of God in our time, the same principle that governed Elisha's life must govern ours.

God's plan. If we desire to see and be part of a great move of God in our time, the same principle that governed Elisha's life must govern ours.

The Heart of the Principle

The Elisha Principle is a spiritual code revealed in the godly character of those who stand firm for the promise of God. It is the mindset that says, "Come hell or high water, I will not tarry here. I'm going to the next level. God has promised the power of breakthrough, and I'm breaking through. He has promised a yoke-crushing anointing, and I will not leave without it."

The budding prophet, Elisha, operated in this principle as he was tested by his mentor, Elijah, at three pivotal points in their relationship. Three times, Elijah told Elisha to stay behind while he (Elijah) moved on. But Elisha, who knew his destiny was connected to Elijah's, refused to leave his mentor's side. Instead, Elisha declared each time: *"As the Lord lives, and as you yourself live, I will not leave you"* (2 Kings 2:2,4,6).

Despite God's call on his life, Elisha faced resistance. Every man or woman destined for a greater revelation of God's power

> Every man or woman destined for a greater revelation of God's power will face resistance.

will face resistance. God allows it and uses it to groom us for His anointing. Our response to resistance is crucial: will we retreat in the face of difficulty or will we advance?

Elisha was tenacious. His response to Elijah's testing revealed his intent, determination, and character—the character of a man molded by the hand of the living God. As long as Elijah was alive and God was with him, Elisha would cleave to his mentor.

Elisha understood that life in the Spirit is marked by movement; stagnancy is evidence of death and decay. Elisha was not interested in clinging to a form or tradition whose usefulness had passed. He knew doing so would accomplish nothing for the purposes of God.

Prepared to Dance

> [Elijah] *found Elisha the son of Shaphat, while he was plowing with twelve pairs of oxen before him, and he with the twelfth. And Elijah passed over to him and threw his mantle on him. He left the oxen and ran after Elijah and said, "Please let me kiss my father and my mother, then I will follow you"* (1 Kings 19:19-20).

Elisha was positioned for the spiritual changing of the guard. He was "found" by Elijah. God's instructions had been clear: *"Jehu the son of Nimshi you shall anoint king over Israel; and Elisha the son of Shaphat of Abel-meholah you shall anoint as prophet in your place"* (1 Kings 19:16).

At Abel-meholah, "the meadow of dancing,"[2] Elisha realized immediately that Elijah had not only what *he* needed, but what *Israel* needed for the next move of God. The "attraction" was mutual: Elijah knew Elisha was the one God had chosen to carry forward the legacy of His anointing.

The two men met on what *I call the path of synchronicity*—the place where connections are made, not by accident, but by meaningful coincidence. Elisha was found because he was ready to be found. He was prepared. He had put his hand to the plow. He made full use of his resources (plowing not with 1 yoke of oxen, but with 12). He held nothing back; he kissed his family goodbye and left with Elijah.

Abel-meholah was the place where Elisha learned to "dance" with the anointed one and his anointing. It was the place where two men of kindred faith connected—the crossroad at which Elisha had to decide whether to stay or go—whether to be content to tarry or compelled to move on with God.

Follow God's Lead

We, too, must recognize when it is time to stay and when it is time to move on, just as the Israelites did on their journey to the Promised Land (see Exod. 40:36-37). When the cloud hovered above the tent of meeting, the people stayed put. But when the cloud moved and Moses cried, *"Rise up, O Lord!"* (Num. 10:35), the Israelites packed up their belongings and followed the Shekinah glory.

> Too often, the greatest hindrance to the move of the Spirit is not the devil, but the Church itself!

Our daily lives are to be guided the same way—by following God's lead. This is also true for the Church; as His Body, we are called to move when He calls us forward. Too often, the greatest hindrance to the move of the Spirit is not the devil, but the Church itself!

This is the season for God's Elishas to cleave to His purposes. Yet, history shows that, at the height of every renewal or revival, many of God's people remain untouched by it. Instead of moving forward with God, they hold on to the "good old days."

In the 1960s and 1970s, many could not accept God's sovereign visitation because He saved young people who wore long hair and faded jeans. Many Pentecostals even believed it was unscriptural for those of other denominations to have a Pentecostal experience. In the decades since, other squabbles have erupted in the family of God, and many have taken issue with the ways in which God has chosen to move among His people.

May God help us to be adaptable and pliable in this hour. May He give us the spirit and determination of Elisha to cleave to His plan and embrace the coming shift. May we ecome a company of Elishas who operate in the double-portion anointing, transform the atmosphere, and leave a blessing behind us!

Endnotes

1. Earle E. Cairns, *Christianity Through the Centuries* (Grand Rapids, MI: Zondervan Publishing House, 1996), 489.

2. Biblesoft's New Exhaustive Strong's Numbers and Concordance with Expanded Greek-Hebrew Dictionary. CD-ROM. Biblesoft, Inc. and International Bible Translators, Inc. s.v. "Abel-meholah," (OT 65).

POINTS TO PONDER

1. In your own words, describe what the Elisha Principle is.

2. "Every man or woman destined for a greater revelation of God's power will face resistance." List the types of things that have provided resistance to you or to other people of God in the past and how these things were or could be overcome.

3. "Too often, the greatest hindrance to the move of the Spirit is not the devil, but the Church itself." Do you agree with this statement? Why or why not?

CHAPTER 2

WHEN THE CLOUD MOVES, MOVE

Jehu the son of Nimshi you shall anoint king over Israel;
and Elisha the son of Shaphat of Abel-meholah you shall
anoint as prophet in your place.
(1 Kings 19:16)

The fiery prophet Elijah received notice from the "Home Office" that his departure from Earth was imminent. His "retirement benefits" would include a whirlwind ride that would take him, not to the grave, but directly to "Headquarters."

But first, some unfinished business needed tending to. Elijah and his protégé, Elisha, would embark on a journey—a literal and spiritual circle that would seal the transfer of the anointing, bring closure to the ministry of Elijah, and establish the double-portion anointing of Elisha. Together, they would travel from Gilgal to Bethel, Jericho, and Jordan.

As we'll see in greater detail later, these places were spiritually significant. These were not random treks, but milestones in God's process of completion that represented and produced in both men (but particularly in Elisha) periods of deeper learning, mastery, surrender, and sacrifice.

Gilgal, Bethel, Jericho, and Jordan would demonstrate Elijah's connection and utter trust in the Most High God. He was a man on the move to the very end, led from place to place by the Holy Spirit. Even in his final earthly days, knowing that his assignment was about to end and someone else would take his place, he braved the uncomfortable winds of transition without complaint.

This was the prophet, Elijah, whose name means "Yah is God."[1] The very message of Elijah's ministry had been written into his name and demonstrated to heathens. In First Kings 18, when Elijah and the priests of Baal faced off at Carmel, the pagans learned firsthand that Yah is truly God and Baal was utterly powerless.

Now, the circular journey of Elijah and his protégé would reveal and thoroughly test the qualities for which God had chosen Elisha. His strength in God would be revealed; his steadfastness would be proven; his ability to persevere would be demonstrated; his willingness to transcend rejection, inconvenience, suffering, delay, and difficulty would be displayed.

Elisha, whose name means, "Yah is salvation," was a type of the salvation purchased for us by Jesus Christ. This salvation crosses national, cultural, social, and denominational lines. In Second Kings 5, we see this truth demonstrated in the healing of Naaman from leprosy through the ministry of Elisha. This healing pictures the welcoming of the Gentile nations into the covenant that would be written in the blood of the King of kings!

But before his ministry could get underway, Elisha would have to follow Elijah's every move; he would have to contend for the inheritance of the double portion.

Yield to God's Agenda

Elijah's departure from earth was unorthodox. His arrival had been equally unusual. When he first appeared on the scene, Elijah seemed to come out of nowhere. Without credentials, ordination papers, or a license to preach, Elijah boldly declared that God would not send rain until Elijah told Him to do so (see 1 Kings 17:1).

With the land in a time of drought, it is easy to imagine that Elijah had his detractors, those who would have seen him as a pompous, arrogant, self-made preacher. "Who is this so-called prophet?" was likely a question that rose to the lips of many. But for those able to discern the Lord's voice, it would have been clear that God was rendering recompense to a rebellious nation.

We live in the same fallen world today. Just as it was easy for some to ignore Elijah's warning, it is easy for people and even nations to get on the wrong side of God's agenda today. How? Simply by resisting the ways in which God chooses to move.

> Just as it was easy for some to ignore Elijah's warning, it is easy for people and even nations to get on the wrong side of God's agenda today.

Much as Elijah did, the Charismatic movement came

seemingly out of nowhere. Many revivals have followed. Through all of them, God touched the hearts of thousands and revealed valuable principles of how He moves and how we can cooperate with Him.

Twentieth-Century Revival Primer

In the early 1900s the fire of Pentecost began to blaze from prayer rooms in Kansas and California. The Azusa Street Revival became a rallying point for the Pentecostal outpouring. Spirit-filled believers began to declare that God was visiting His people with a "latter rain" of glory preceding the coming of the Lord.

The Book of Acts came alive! Yet, this visitation met with resistance and persecution. Over the years, I've heard stories from seniors at our church who were threatened even to the point of death! Many were asked to leave their own churches because, in the eyes of unbelieving leadership, they had embraced heretical doctrine. This occurred in America, Canada, areas of Europe, Norway, Sweden, Australia, and New Zealand.

As strong as the opposition was, the Pentecostal movement continued. The Assemblies of God were birthed during this outpouring. Many who later came to be known as great men and women of God were considered by Evangelical fundamentalists in that day to be heretics and troublemakers. People such as Charles Price, Smith Wigglesworth, John Lake, the Bosworths, Mary Woodworth-Etter, and Aimee Semple McPherson (to name just a few) ministered with great power and authority and met with strong resistance.

In the late 1940s, God visited a small group of farmers in North Battleford, Saskatchewan, with a glorious outpouring of the Spirit, which became known as the Latter Rain.[2] Spontaneous praise, worship, and prophecy were earmarks of this revival, which started with a few people in a frozen, isolated region and spread like wildfire.

God again visited the Earth with power and glory in the late 1960s. Thousands of young men and women, disgusted with "the establishment," found refuge in drugs, sex, rock music, and communal living. Astoundingly, with no apparent prompting, they began to call upon the name of Jesus. He set them free from bondages and sin and filled them with His Spirit.

Thus, the "Jesus People" were born.[3] As they continued to call upon the Lord, their movement became the catalyst for the Charismatic Renewal, which led to a sovereign visitation spanning every denomination in Christendom. It was common to find Lutherans, Methodists, Presbyterians, Catholics, Episcopalians, and others gathering at citywide rallies to praise the name of Jesus.

Many thousands were converted and set free. Many were healed of diseases; many more received the baptism of the Holy Spirit (with the evidence of speaking in other tongues) as the early Church did on the day of Pentecost (see Acts 2:1-4). Prayer meetings became the focal point of many churches and for a while, the born-again experience gained media attention from coast to coast.

> God only honors those who live what they preach.

Celebrities, politicians, and entertainers began to testify of being born again. Most were sincere; a few, however, claimed the experience for the sake of acceptance and personal gain. Sadly, this weakened the Church's testimony because, although the fanfare was lively, there was no anointing behind it. (God only honors those who live what they preach.)

> The Church is at the forefront of spiritual activity in the natural realm.

God continues to move through the Church. Beginning in the 1990s, the world experienced fresh outpourings in Toronto (the Toronto Blessing), Pensacola (the Brownsville Revival), and southern California (the Anaheim Vineyard Renewal). Some of these revivals continue as of this writing, and many lives have been impacted.

The Church is at the forefront of spiritual activity in the natural realm. It is the *Body* of Christ, the corporate vessel through which God moves to accomplish His will in the earth.

The Trappings of Transition

In every move of God, reactions vary widely. Thousands attend; many bring friends and loved ones; people are healed, delivered, and transformed. Yet many take issue: they are either outright opposed or disappointed, as though God's move failed to live up to their expectations of what He would do.

The presence of opposition or discouragement in the wake of spiritual movement is not a new phenomenon. Remember Elijah?

After the all-out showdown in which he slew hundreds of prophets of Baal, Elijah cowered at a threat from wicked Jezebel and fled for his life. (See First Kings 18 and 19.)

Just as Elijah was ready to pack it in, God sent an angel with food (see 1 Kings 19:5-6). Elijah ate and ran to Mount Horeb. When he arrived there, he and God had a "church service" in which God preached an illustrated sermon using wind, earthquakes, and fire to get His point across. Elijah complained that he was the only one left in all Israel who was hungry for more of God. But God's records indicated there were at least 7,000 others! (See First Kings 19:18.)

It was at Horeb, the Mount of God, that Elijah received a heavenly perspective on the situation. God showed him that he was not alone in his faith. Elijah was surrounded by idol worshipers, yet there were many other passionate followers of God besides him.

We, too, need a heavenly perspective that looks outward from self to see the larger picture. It is important that we hear what the Lord is saying and perceive the workings of His power and grace in the hearts of His faithful.

> We, too, need a heavenly perspective that looks outward from self to see the larger picture.

Elijah thought he was alone, but there was a faithful remnant in Israel who had not bowed their knees to Baal. God had 7,000 He could count on. *Seven* is the number of perfection. *One thousand* is a number symbolizing completeness. There was a perfect and complete company of believers worshiping the one true God.

Among the 7,000 was Elisha, God's answer to Elijah's depression. Elisha was also God's provision for Israel and the ideal successor to Elijah.

Joy, No Matter What

Elijah would spend the remainder of his days preparing Elisha to replace him.

In Chapter 1, we learned about Elisha's hometown, *Abel-meholah* or "meadow of the dance." Dance is festive and joyous; Elisha lived in a place that was a picture of rejoicing! Paul the apostle tells us to *"rejoice always"* (1 Thess. 5:16) and *"rejoice in the Lord always"* (Phil. 4:4). God is always looking for people who live with a joyful attitude—people who will look to Him and rejoice, not necessarily *for* all things, but *in* all things. God wants to use a people who will express His joy.

> God is always looking for people who live with a joyful attitude.

Abel-meholah is also a crossroads, a place where difficult decisions are made and challenges are faced. Some of my close friends and I came to the Lord in the early 1970s. Many of us have experienced a good deal of adversity and tribulation in the years since. Yet God continues to teach us that we can rejoice in Him. We have learned that steadfast joy protects our hearts. When we *"hope against hope"* (Rom. 4:18) as Abraham did, God invests Himself in us through the hardships we face!

James 1:2 tells us to *"consider it all joy"* when the going gets tough. God is preparing us for great things. We can't allow ourselves to be swayed or deceived by the Baals of our day. Manmade idols and promises of the easy life feed on the sinister spirit of this age.

> We are called to endure for the sake of our faith in Christ; in doing so, we will reap great reward.

We are called to endure for the sake of our faith in Christ; in doing so, we will reap great reward. The Lord might allow us to encounter difficulties; but like Elisha, we can make our home in Abel-meholah, where God will turn our *"mourning into dancing"* (Ps. 30:11).

Working in His Fields

God sent Elijah to Elisha. When Elijah found his "replacement," he (Elisha) was plowing a field with 12 pair of oxen (see 1 Kings 19:19-20). In other words, Elisha served a dual role: he labored and gave orders. He plowed with one pair of oxen and oversaw 11 other pairs. Why was Elisha working so hard? He was plowing and preparing the ground for his father to sow.

When Jesus was 12, He wandered from His parents and went to His Father's house. When His worried parents found Him, He explained that He had to be about His Father's work (see Luke 2:49). What was Jesus doing? He was plowing the field of His heart and mind; He was making room for the precious seed of the Word. The Word reaped a perfect harvest in Him, for He was and is the Word.

Elisha was plowing, and by example leading 11 others in the same direction. This was part of his preparation for ministry. *Twelve* is the number of governmental perfection (12 tribes of Israel; 12 apostles). Elisha had to be thorough; he had to become skilled in managing his affairs before he could receive Elijah's mantle.

We can't move forward until we finish what we've started.

The fact that Elisha was plowing with the twelfth of the 11 pair of oxen signified that he was bringing the work to completion. Before we enter the next season of Church history (or any transition), we must bring to completion the season we are in. We can't move forward until we finish what we've started.

Notice that, although Elisha oversaw the operation in the field, he was not concerned with being center stage; he was getting his hands dirty with everybody else, preparing the ground for seed. Likewise, God is causing certain of His servants to plow together in preparation for the sowing of precious seed. They have not been in the forefront; the public isn't aware of them. But God is. These faithful laborers are part of a team that is plowing together, faithful to do what their hands find to do. They are serving wholeheartedly in Father's house. They have not *"despised the day of small things"* (Zech. 4:10); they are believing for greater things in the days ahead.

For some, visions and dreams have tarried for a season. We need to be reminded that God is not slow regarding His promises. He will perform what He says. As we plow together and break up the fallow ground, God will bless our labors and in His time give us what we desire. The words of Habakkuk are fitting:

> *Though the fig tree should not blossom, and there be no fruit on the vines, though the yield of the olive should fail and the fields produce no food, though the flock should be cut off from the fold and there be no cattle in the stalls, yet I will exult in the Lord, I will rejoice in the God of my salvation. The Lord God is my strength, and He has made my feet like hinds' feet, and makes me walk on my high places* (Habakkuk 3:17-19).

Endnotes

1. James Orr, ed., *International Standard Bible Encyclopedia* (Chicago: The Howard-Severence Co., 1915), s.v. "Elijah."

2. Randall Balmer, *Encyclopedia of Evangelicalism* (Waco, TX: Baylor University Press, 2004), 397.

3. Earle E. Cairns, *Christianity Through the Centuries* (Grand Rapids, MI: Zondervan Publishing House, 1996), 489.

POINTS TO PONDER

1. "Elijah thought he was alone…." Have you ever felt alone? Read John 14:18 and Hebrews 13:5b.

2. "*Rejoice in the Lord always*" (Phil. 4:4). God is always looking for people who live with a joyful attitude." Take the time to write down and even speak aloud some things you are thankful for.

Chapter 3

From Gilgal to Father's House

And it came about when the Lord was about to take up Elijah by a whirlwind to heaven, that Elijah went with Elisha from Gilgal. Elijah said to Elisha, "Stay here please, for the Lord has sent me as far as Bethel." But Elisha said, "As the Lord lives and as you yourself live, I will not leave you." So they went down to Bethel.
(2 Kings 2:1-2)

After he found Elisha, but before his whirlwind ride to Heaven, Elijah made his final rounds to the places where he had established ministry. He and Elisha started this wrap-up at Gilgal, a place that has great significance in the redemptive history of Israel and also has meaning for our own redemptive history in Christ.

Gilgal means "circle of stones."[1] In Joshua 4, the nation of Israel set up 12 stones in the midst of the Jordan River and 12 stones on the dry land as a memorial to the Lord. These stones would remind future generations that the Lord had enabled Israel to cross the river on dry ground and had "rolled away" the reproach of Egypt.

It was at Gilgal that the Lord instructed Joshua to circumcise all the males who were born in the wilderness (see Josh. 5:2). Circumcision was the sign of the Abrahamic Covenant, as the Lord explained to Abraham:

> *This is My covenant, which you shall keep, between Me and you and your descendants after you: every male among you shall be circumcised.... But an uncircumcised male who is not circumcised in the flesh of his foreskin, that person shall be cut off from his people; he has broken My covenant* (Genesis 17:10,14).

Circumcision was the initiation rite into the covenant community of Israel and the sole form of identification with the God of Abraham. The circumcision of the men at Gilgal fulfilled the conditions of the Abrahamic Covenant and foreshadowed the circumcision of our hearts in Christ.

Paul tells us in Colossians 2:11: *"In Him you were also circumcised with a circumcision made without hands, in the removal of the body of the flesh by the circumcision of Christ...."* This is a glorious truth! When we receive and embrace the sacrifice of Christ by faith, we automatically enter into the provisions of the New Covenant, of which Christ is the Mediator. He sacrificed

His life for the redemption of all transgressions resulting from the first covenant.

A New-Covenant Gilgal

Through Christ we received an eternal inheritance. The blessings of this covenant were not valid until after Christ's death. Legally speaking, this is true today. When a person bequeaths property in a will, the beneficiary receives it only after the person dies.

By the circumcision of Christ we have been translated out of the kingdom of darkness and delivered from the reproach of sin, shame, and woundedness. The pain of circumcision experienced by the sons of Israel at Gilgal (as initiation under the Old Covenant) is nothing compared to what Christ suffered on Calvary in order to initiate the New Covenant. It was there that our sin was exchanged for His righteousness.

> The circumcision of our hearts occurs at the moment of repentance. This is our new beginning.

The circumcision of our hearts occurs at the moment of repentance. This is our new beginning. When we confess our sinfulness to Christ and accept His substitutionary death, we are born of the Spirit. We are at our spiritual Gilgal. For Elisha, Gilgal was the beginning level of his testing. If he had stopped there, he would not have received the double portion. Neither is Gilgal our endpoint!

On the day of Pentecost Peter said, *"Repent, and...**be baptized...**"* (Acts 2:38). While our hearts are circumcised inwardly, water baptism reveals this reality outwardly. The word *baptize* in the Greek means "to immerse, submerge; to make overwhelmed (*i.e.,* fully wet)."[2] In the Book of Acts, the only people who were baptized were those who first encountered the Lord Jesus Christ by repentance and confession.

Following the Charismatic Renewal and any other move of God, large numbers of people enter into a "Gilgal" experience with the Lord; they testify of being born again. Too many who have come to Christ have not fully understood the Gilgal experience and have never progressed beyond that point. They testify of *how* God saved them and what He saved them *from,* but they never realize what He saved them *for!*

> Salvation is more than just being saved, healed, and filled with the Holy Ghost.

Proverbs 29:18 tells us that without a progressive vision, the people live carelessly. Salvation is more than just being saved, healed, and filled with the Holy Ghost. Gilgal should be the place where our "excess baggage" begins to be stripped away so that we can move in the anointing. It is the place where we realize that we can go forward with God because we are no longer under condemnation (see Rom. 8:1).

Gilgal should be the place where the door closes on the past and we begin to mature spiritually, individually, and as a local body. While many fine ministries have been raised up in the years since the Charismatic movement began, some have been founded on a limited understanding of the covenant. As a result, leaders have re-produced their lack of understanding in others. Shallow preaching and teaching have too often produced shallow converts.

We need to plumb the depths of the Gilgal experience; and then we need to move on.

From Gilgal to Fellowship

We need to be taught from the moment of repentance what God has in store for us. There has been only one purpose, *one* program, and *one* will in the eternal counsels of the Most High since before the world began.

God's motive is absolutely pure and stems from His love and grace. As Charismatics, some of us desperately need our perspectives broadened. If we focus solely on Gilgal and our conversion experience, we risk emphasizing one aspect of the truth to the exclusion of the whole truth.

> If we focus solely on Gilgal and our conversion experience, we risk emphasizing one aspect of the truth to the exclusion of the whole truth.

To do so is to give the impression that being saved and having all your prayers answered are all there is to Christianity. The "me-oriented" age in which we live has affected not only our lifestyles, but also much of the preaching we hear. The truth is that the world does not revolve around any one of us, any denomination, or any particular experience in God. On the contrary; all things revolve around Christ and Him alone.

God saves us for more than our comfort; He saves us so we can enter into fellowship with Him. Christ is the hub around which all things revolve. Without Him at the center, we will lose our balance and run off course. To fully appreciate the truth of fellowship with God, we must have an understanding of the basic nature of God Himself. It is the Fatherhood of God that drives His activity in the life of every believer.

> Christ is the hub around which all things revolve. Without Him at the center, we will lose our balance and run off course.

The Fatherhood of God implies a paternal emphasis in His interaction with us. God has intended to have many sons and daughters in His one Son, the Lord Jesus Christ. We, as God's children, are to share the kind of relationship with the Father that Christ enjoyed while He walked the earth. As with the first son He created in Eden, God's desire has been to walk in the *"cool of the day"* (Gen. 3:8) with each of His children.

By growing in fellowship with the Father, we grow in service as well. Gilgal was the place where the reproach—the oppressive yoke of Egypt—was removed. When we are saved, the Lord removes from us the yoke of sin. When that burden is lifted, the heaviness of sin leaves us. (See Romans 6:5-7.)

However, while God delivers us from the yoke of sin, He desires us to be yoked to His Son. The *Zondervan Pictorial Encyclopedia* tells us that the word *yoke* refers to a heavy wooden frame used to tie together two draft animals (such as oxen); the yoked animals can then successfully pull heavy loads such as plows and carts.

In Matthew 11:30 Jesus says His *"yoke is easy"* and His *"burden is light."* If we want to have fellowship with Him, we have to be yoked to Him! Too many believers have come to Gilgal, but failed to put their heads in the yoke. But that is exactly what servant-hood is—sharing the yoke with Jesus.

The Nature of the Yoke

What exactly is this yoke? It's the will of the Father! When God put Adam in the Garden, He put him to work. When Jesus walked the earth, He said: *"My food is to do the will of Him who sent Me, and to accomplish His work"* (John 4:34).

If we aren't serving God, we are serving ourselves. Whether we realize it or not, we all wear yokes. We are either slaves to sin or slaves to righteousness. The yoke of self leads to slavery and bondage, while the yoke of Jesus leads to liberty and freedom.

Remember, Gilgal is the place of beginnings. If we never fully enter in, and continue clinging to the yoke of self-centeredness, we will remain there the rest of our lives. Unfortunately, some Christian media encourage a self-focused, "get all you can" attitude. But Jesus' message is not "get all you can"; it's "lose all you have"! According to Him, that's the only way to find real life (see Matt. 10:39).

> We are either slaves to sin or slaves to righteousness.

Elisha wore the yoke. He was committed. Why Elijah encouraged him to remain at Gilgal is a matter open to speculation.

Perhaps God was perfecting Elisha's faith by testing it as Jesus had done with the Syrophoenician woman in Matthew 15:22-28. When this woman asked Jesus' help for her daughter, He at first disregarded her request. On the face of it, Jesus' response seemed cruel. He boldly declared that *"the children's bread"* (the blessings of His ministry) was reserved for the *"house of Israel." He even* went on to call the Gentiles "dogs"!

Still, the woman did not despair. She replied, humbly, that "even dogs pick up crumbs that fall from the table." As a result, her faith was rewarded. She received the desire of her heart: the healing of her daughter.

It may be that God was allowing a similar challenge in the life of Elisha. After all, God had big plans for the prophet and was not about to hand him the ministry on a silver platter; Elisha was going to have to pursue it!

And he did. Elisha would not be satisfied to stay at Gilgal, and we shouldn't be either. That is not to say that we are dissatisfied with the blessing of the Lord. Instead, we are *unsatisfied* because the taste of good things to come makes us hungry for more. Elisha had that hunger; he knew that to receive from Elijah all that God had for him, he would have to fully engage the Gilgal experience and then move on.

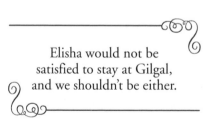

Elisha would not be satisfied to stay at Gilgal, and we shouldn't be either.

When the cloud permeates the meeting in the camp, we should rest and remain; but when the cloud moves, we need to pack up the tent and follow.

Submission and Obedience

The topic of submission to authority always attracts attention. Over the years, there has been some excellent teaching in this area; there have also been some unhealthy and unhelpful approaches.

The key to submission is demonstrated by the relationship between Elijah and Elisha. In fact, submission is the essence of the Elisha Principle in action: what Elisha submitted to was the anointing! If the anointing had lifted (due to abuse of authority or some other form of sin), then the blessing of the Lord in Elijah's life would have been removed. At that point, Elisha's submission would have rightly ended.

In Second Kings 2:2, Elijah revealed to Elisha that the Lord was sending him to Bethel. He knew his time to depart was coming and the Lord was going to remove him in the whirlwind. What he didn't know was exactly where and when it would happen. It is apparent that God led Elijah one step at a time. Once he obeyed a step, God gave him further instruction.

Submission is the essence of the Elisha Principle in action.

Often, we want to know the end of the story at the beginning. We want God to reveal His complete blueprint before we've even taken our first steps. God didn't deal with His people that way in the Scriptures; we needn't expect Him to do so with us. Instead, we are called to respond in faith to whatever light we have. Then God will give us more.

When Abraham left Ur of the Chaldees, he had no idea where he was going; he just knew he had to obey God. If God had told Abraham all that was coming, he might have been overwhelmed at the prospect and been tempted to shrink away. We need to know enough to keep us moving forward. Then we need only obey one step at a time.

Between a Rock and a Hard Place

The second stop in Elijah's journey with Elisha was Bethel, another historically important site.

In Genesis 28, Jacob, the heir apparent of the covenant, fled the wrath of Esau, the brother who had threatened his life. On his journey toward Haran, Jacob stopped to camp for the night. He had no pillow; he laid his head on a rock and quickly fell asleep.

Jacob slept at Mount Moriah, a place where God's glory had already been seen. It was where Abraham had come to sacrifice Isaac. Now, Isaac's own son would experience the glory of God at that very place.

Jacob began to dream and received a revelation from God. He saw a ladder reaching to an open Heaven, with angels ascending to and descending from the presence of the Lord. Then God renewed the covenant promises He'd made to Abraham, unconditionally committing Himself to Jacob (see Gen. 28:13-14). He also assured Jacob of His protection and the fulfillment of His promises. Any consciousness Jacob had of being separated from God was gone!

Upon waking, Jacob said, *"Surely the Lord is in this place…"* (Gen. 28:16). Suddenly, Jacob was aware that God was present, not only above him, but with him. He also witnessed the ministry of angels, which had gone unnoticed by him to that point. With his head on that rock the night before, Jacob had both lost consciousness (to sleep) and had his consciousness expanded by God.

Jacob built an altar to the Lord and named the place *Bethel,* meaning "house of God."[3] The Bethel revelation is very important for the Body of Christ. The apostle Peter said that we (the Church) are being built up as a *"spiritual house,"* a Bethel, if you will, *"for a holy priesthood"* (1 Pet. 2:5). The writer of the Book of Hebrews said that Christ is the Head of His Father's house—and we are the house! (See Hebrews 3:6.) The Church is Bethel; we are the temple of the living God!

> The Church is Bethel; we are the temple of the living God!

God has purposed to build His house. He placed a wise Master Builder over the construction and gave Him skilled artisans and craftsmen to oversee the work. When Christ ascended to Heaven, apostles, prophets, evangelists, pastors, and teachers began to fulfill their roles in the overall blueprint of the Church. These members of the fivefold ministry are assigned to help the house function effectively (see Eph. 4:11-12).

The local church is the visible expression of God's Covenant; it is *the* covenant community. In the local church, the ladder of Christ's presence touches Heaven and releases the blessings of the

Father to those in need. It is also a place of development and training. The local church functioning according to the New Testament pattern is the best seminary in the world.

Commitment and accountability are essential to growth—individually and in the church setting. In many circles there has been an unhealthy emphasis on personalities and ministries; this has produced followers of men rather than followers of God. As a result, many consider the words of these leaders infallible without searching the Scripture for themselves.

> Commitment and accountability are essential to growth—individually and in the church setting.

Paul struggled with the church at Corinth over this very issue. All of the gifts of the Spirit were in operation, and supernatural manifestations were commonplace, but some considered themselves to be followers of Apollos, others believed Peter, and still others were convinced that to be really mature, you had to follow Paul. *"Has Christ been divided?"* Paul asked in First Corinthians 1:13.

How grievous this kind of idolatry is to the Lord. Many ministries once used mightily by God are no longer in the forefront. Some leaders lost sight of who really heads the Church. They began believing their own press releases. As a result, God withdrew the anointing.

If we seek to develop a following and promote our own ministries, we are building our kingdoms instead of His Kingdom. This will always produce casualties. Highly regarded men and women of God will fall into sin, and many of their followers will stumble and fall.

These things ought not to be. God wants to do great things in the earth. We need to learn from past mistakes. We must not make gods of mere people. Only God is God.

> If we seek to develop a following and promote our own ministries, we are building our kingdoms instead of His Kingdom.

The Critical Local Church

In the New Testament and especially in the Book of Acts, we see that when people were converted, God placed them in fellowship with other believers in a local church. God's pattern has not changed. If we want to see the kind of power demonstrated in the Book of Acts, we need to follow the pattern it reveals.

Some believers wander like lone rangers for years without being grafted into a local church. This spiritual malady starts at Gilgal for those who forget to get in the yoke with Jesus. Waiting to find the "perfect church," they fail to recognize their own imperfections and rebellion. They fear allowing God to smooth out their rough edges in the fire of fellowship with other imperfect people. Therefore, they never experience being transformed into the image of Christ.

At Bethel, we are under an open Heaven; we have access to realms of endless, invisible supply. But Bethel is also a craggy place; to get under that open Heaven you've got to be willing to climb the rough side of the mountain. Getting there will cost you something; much of the cost (and much of the reward) will come through a new dimension of relationship with others, mentors and peers alike.

> Some of us prefer to avoid the sharpening and smoothing that comes from authentic relationships.

Some of us prefer to avoid the sharpening and smoothing that comes from authentic relationships. Others fail to plug into a local church because they are lazy. Getting out of bed on Sunday morning seems too hard. These dear people, however, are often the same ones who continually seek private counsel to help them overcome their problems. I have decided that if a person wants my counsel, he must sit through at least two consecutive weeks of my preaching. Those who make the effort to really absorb the preached Word often find that their problems are solved without any counseling!

We need to come back to the foundation of the house. The local church, when it functions as it should, will minister to all the needs of God's people. If this is not happening, either the necessary equipping of believers is lacking or the believers are immature and rebellious—or both.

Imperfections are many, but be of good cheer. The Spirit of God is stirring the local church. The proper emphasis is being restored. The local church is called to be the center for renewal, revival, and restoration in the lives of God's people.

Large para-church organizations that operate outside the auspices of a particular church or denomination are not as prone to overshadowing the local church as in years past. This is not to say that these organizations are unbiblical. Some have done a tremendous work for God where the Church has failed to meet a need. But it is criti-

> The local church, when it functions as it should, will minister to all the needs of God's people.

cally important that the local church not become a side issue. A para-church organization is not intended to be an end in itself—it is a feeder program back to the local church.

His Kingdom Come

God isn't committed to building our kingdoms; He is committed to building *His*. We need to lay our kingdoms at His feet. It is His house that He chooses to build.

God is building a mighty army of flesh-and-blood believers functioning according to the proper working of each individual part. The foundation of the house is the Rock on which Jacob slept: Christ and Christ alone.

In Revelation 21:22-23 we have a picture of the Church in all her glory:

> *I saw no temple in it, for the Lord God the Almighty and the Lamb are its temple. And the city has no need of the sun or of the moon to shine on it, for the glory of God has illumined it, and its lamp is the Lamb.*

What is the Spirit revealing in these verses about the Church? A temple is a manmade structure; the Church is a holy temple conceived in the mind of God before the world began. Man

> God isn't committed to building our kingdoms; He is committed to building *His.*

cannot construct a dwelling place for the Lord. Heaven is His throne and the earth His footstool. Nothing we construct could possibly contain Him. Instead, He has brought forth a Church through the finished work of Christ. That Church is intended by God to express His manifold grace (see 1 Pet. 4:10).

The sun and moon are the natural bodies by which God has illuminated our world. In God's spiritual house there is no room for natural light. Natural methods do not produce supernatural results. If you begin in the flesh, you end up with…flesh! If unbelievers are attracted to anything other than the light of Christ, it is because we Christians are failing to accurately reflect His light.

Just as the moon reflects the sun, we are to shine with the brightness of Christ's glory, reflecting His radiance in the midst of a dark world. Jesus said that we are the light of the world (see Matt. 5:14). *"The path of the righteous is like the light of dawn, that shines brighter and brighter until the full day"* (Prov. 4:18).

In the days ahead, I believe God desires to move in a greater way to bring a fuller manifestation of the glory of His presence. An old Pentecostal chorus expresses this thought well:

> "There's a mighty glory coming, and it's coming down today, and it's coming here to stay. There's a mighty glory coming, and it's coming from the presence of the Lord!"

Just as Elisha was determined to follow Elijah to Bethel, so we must embrace the Bethel revelation and move on with God. The local church is where it's happening in the days ahead. Let's be sure we are plugged in—empowered by His means and for His glory!

Endnotes

1. Herbert Lockyer, Sr., ed., *Nelson's Illustrated Bible Dictionary*, (Nashville: Thomas Nelson Publishers, 1986), s.v. "Gilgal."

2. Biblesoft's New Exhaustive Strong's Numbers and Concordance with Expanded Greek-Hebrew Dictionary. CD-ROM. Biblesoft, Inc. and International Bible Translators, Inc. s.v. "baptize" (NT 907).

3. Biblesoft's New Exhaustive Strong's Numbers and Concordance with Expanded Greek-Hebrew Dictionary. CD-ROM. Biblesoft, Inc. and International Bible Translators, Inc. s.v. "Bethel," (OT 1008).

Points to Ponder

1. "Some believers wander like lone rangers for years without being grafted into a local church. ...Waiting to find the "perfect church," they fail to recognize their own imperfections and rebellion. They fear allowing God to smooth out their rough edges in the fire of fellowship with other imperfect people. Therefore, they never experience being transformed into the image of Christ."

   Does this describe you? Are you committed to, involved in, and accountable to a local body of believers? Or are you the lone ranger, trying to do it all alone, unattached to other believers?

2. What does Gilgal represent? What does Bethel represent? And where do you see yourself in this journey?

3. "Heaven is His throne and the earth His footstool. Nothing we construct could possibly contain Him." Think about that visual image for a minute. Heaven is His throne, and the earth is His footstool. Wow! What an awesome God we serve! Take a minute and just lavish praise on the King of the universe.

CHAPTER 4

WE ARE STANDING ON
HOLY GROUND

The sons of the prophets who were at Bethel came out to
Elisha and said to him, "Do you know that the Lord will
take away your master from over you today?" And he said,
"Yes, I know; be still." Elijah said to him, "Elisha, please
stay here, for the Lord has sent me to Jericho." But he said,
"As the Lord lives, and as you yourself live, I will not leave
you." So they came to Jericho.
(2 Kings 2:3-4)

In the early history of the prophetic ministry of Israel, "schools of the prophets" or "sons of the prophets" popped up. The earliest mention of such groups is found in the Book of First Samuel.

Judging by the names of these groups, one might think that Samuel started them to develop or train future prophets. Yet historical records reveal that these men were followers of the prophets who acted as more of a support group. They were men who wanted to be part of what was happening. We have no indication in the biblical record that God ever called any of His prophets from these groups. Instead, the call of God to the prophetic office remained one of sovereign election.

In Elisha's case, these men posed a problem. They typify a malady common today: it is the tendency by some in the Charismatic stream to seek after the "latest" revelation or the "newest" truth. Sadly, many of these people seem always to be learning but never developing knowledge of the truth (see 2 Tim. 3:7). They are carried along by *"every wind of doctrine"* (Eph. 4:14). Always searching for the "deep" things of God, their lives are marked by shallowness. By the time they ought to be teachers, they themselves need to be taught the elementary principles of God (see Heb. 5:12).

Nix the Naysayers

Elisha had been prepared for the ministry by Elijah and word had gotten around that Elijah was about to be removed. Perhaps the sons of the prophets heard it from Elijah himself. Whatever the origin, the story began to spread and the sons of the prophets tried to use it to stir doubt in Elisha's heart.

Elisha did not approve of the sons of the prophets; nor was he distracted by them (see 2 Kings 2:3,5). He simply told them to keep quiet. Elisha was hungry for what God was doing and would not be deterred. He realized that these men did not know what he knew. While *he* understood the *why* of God's plan, they failed to perceive what was really happening.

Elisha would not second-guess God's plan on the basis of anything the sons of the prophets said or did. He knew the moment was near for the transfer of the anointing. He had gotten a taste of God's ways and would not settle for anything less. Elisha had peered into the invisible realm and could not be content with what satisfied the

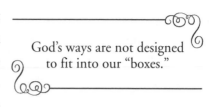

God's ways are not designed to fit into our "boxes."

sons of the prophets. There was no going back; Elisha was determined to be exactly where he needed to be, doing precisely what he was supposed to do.

The lesson here for all of us is: There will always be those who try to hold us back. Afraid of the unknown, they believe it their duty to discourage others from venturing forward in faith.

The arguments such "discouragers" make for not moving forward are usually excuses designed to conceal their own insecurities. This happens in the pews of the church; sadly, it also happens in the pulpit. Preachers who are uncomfortable with the move of God's Spirit often quench the Spirit altogether. They play God and prevent their congregations from moving into greater freedom. Driven by fear, they work overtime to make sure things don't get too "out of hand."

The problem is that God's ways are not designed to fit into our "boxes." The Kingdom will always manifest itself with power. Wherever Jesus went, people were healed, delivered, and set free. Some of them made noise and got excited. Had some of our present-day preachers been there, they might well have asked Jesus to take the "disturbance" down the street.

The only cure for this fear is honest self-examination in the presence of the Lord. The Word of God is not void of power, but we can make it appear that way. Without the Spirit, the Word is lifeless. We need to learn how to appraise things by the Spirit of God. He abides within us and leads us into all truth.

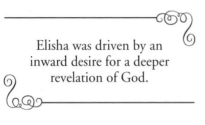

Elisha was driven by an inward desire for a deeper revelation of God.

The sons of the prophets were void of spiritual depth and understanding—they were trying to hold Elisha back from doing what he knew he had to do. He was extreme and fanatical in their eyes. They carefully couched their words by appearing to embrace Elisha's best interests. "Don't you know your master is going to be taken from over you today?" they asked. "Aren't you going a bit too far with this thing, Elisha? Don't you know you will only be hurt in the end?" (See Second Kings 2:5.)

Of course Elisha was being neither foolish nor presumptuous. He had already counted the cost of his commitment to God and Elijah. Therefore, Elisha responded by telling them to mind their own business. They couldn't discern his motives. They couldn't even see past their own noses—let alone understand what was in Elisha's heart.

Elisha was driven by an inward desire for a deeper revelation of God. It was a consuming passion. It was his "magnificent obsession." Even Elijah couldn't persuade Elisha to tarry at Bethel (see 2 Kings 2:4).

Beyond Bethel to Jericho

Bethel is the house of God…the Church…the place of commitment and accountability. We have stressed the importance of being part of a local expression of the Body of Christ. However, it is not enough to tithe and be on the membership roles of a local church.

It isn't even enough to be present at all the meetings. Too many people in this hour are playing church instead of *being* the Church. They become permanent but immovable fixtures.

> Too many people in this hour are playing church instead of *being* the Church.

Playing church keeps the Body of Christ weak in critical areas. The house of God is not a social club; it is the Body of Christ, *"the fullness of Him who fills all in all"* (Eph. 1:23). Just as we should not be content to remain at Gilgal, we cannot be content to remain with the sons of the prophets at Bethel when God is calling us farther along.

As the generation of Elisha, we need to see beyond the outward appearance of religion and beyond a "religious" lifestyle. We must determine to fulfill our ministry one to another as God intended.

Everyone in the Body has a place and a ministry to fulfill. The Body is a living organism attached to a living Head, and He is ordering all things after the counsel of His will (see Eph. 1:11). As a living organism, the Body is to function according to the proper working of each individual part. If your feet are bound, you cannot go anywhere; if your liver is impaired, toxicity will set in and death will eventually ensue.

When the Lord saves us and places us in His Church, we are to come out of the pews and function in our particular God-ordained capacities. The prophet Amos has a fitting word of caution against becoming stagnant pew-sitters: *"Woe to those who are at ease in Zion…"* (Amos 6:1). We need to shake ourselves out of our comfort zones and become loosed from our captivity (see Isa. 52:1-2). We need to become aligned with the vibrant *life* of the Church.

> When the Lord saves us and places us in His Church, we are to come out of the pews and function in our particular God-ordained capacities.

God has called us to follow Elijah beyond the high ground of Bethel, to the deep valley of Jericho. It is the arena of warfare, the place where battles will be fought and strongholds will be taken down. We'll see that although Jericho is a low place we would rather not enter, it is also the place of ultimate victory—not because we will "make things happen," but because, if we will simply show up and obey Him, we will witness God's power!

Yes. It would be easier to remain at Bethel, enjoying the security it offers and avoiding confrontations with the enemy; but if we want all that God has, we must press on to Jericho (even if Elijah tries to persuade us otherwise)!

Warfare, Jericho-Style

Scripture shows the spiritual significance of Jericho. We begin in Joshua 5 with an occurrence known as a *theophany*. It is a theological term used to describe an appearance by the Son of God before His earthly incarnation. In this case, Joshua encountered an individual whom the Scriptures refer to as the *"captain of the host of the Lord"* (Josh. 5:14-15).

Why would Joshua encounter the Captain of the hosts of the Lord? And why is He wearing military apparel? Does His appearance speak of war? And if so, why? God had given the Promised Land to the Israelites—surely they wouldn't have to fight for it! Yet Psalm 24:8 reminds us that the Lord is a warrior, *"mighty in battle."*

The individual Joshua encountered not only wanted to know whether Joshua was on His side, but He also had a drawn sword in His hand to encourage the right decision. Joshua was commanded to remove his sandals because he was on holy ground. The Captain then gave him detailed instructions concerning how the sons of Israel were to capture Jericho.

Jericho was the first city in the Promised Land to be conquered by Israel under the leadership of Joshua (see Joshua 6). It is fascinating to learn that no weapons were used to demolish the walls of Jericho. Instead, the Israelites marched, blew trumpets, and shouted to achieve victory.

What kind of army would march around a city once a day for six days; then march seven times on the seventh day and shout the walls down? God's army! Can you imagine how perplexed the people of Jericho were as they watched the children of Israel?

At Jericho, Israel received an object lesson from the Lord: They learned that if they were to possess the land, they would have to follow the Lord's strategy. Only then would they achieve an absolute and completely supernatural victory.

The Church can draw on the many truths Jericho illumines. One of these involves the name *Jericho,* which means "fragrant"[1] Spiritually speaking, fragrance is a reminder of the altar of incense in the tabernacle of Moses and in the heavenly tabernacle (see Exod. 30:1-10; Rev. 8:3). Incense symbolizes praise, prayer, and worship. In the tabernacle of Moses, the fragrance of incense passed through the thin veil concealing the Ark of the Covenant and ascended above the Mercy Seat to the Shekinah cloud. The angel in Revelation 8 also holds a vial of incense, representing the prayers and worship of the saints.

> Since our warfare is spiritual, our weapons and strategy must be spiritual as well.

But, how does this relate to warfare? In this way: At the heart of the Christian life, there is an ongoing battle. Paul explained that the battle is not physical, but spiritual: *"We wrestle not against flesh and blood, but against principalities, against powers..."* (Eph. 6:12 KJV).

Since our warfare is spiritual, our weapons and strategy must be spiritual as well. *"The weapons of our warfare are not carnal, but mighty through God to the pulling down of strong holds..."* (2 Cor. 10:4 KJV). The walls of Jericho formed a physical stronghold with spiritual significance; and those walls were *pulled down*—through the Israelites' obedience and willingness to do the seemingly silly, non-military things God asked!

The Charismatic approach to praise, worship, and warfare is one of the most exciting aspects of modern renewal history. The lifting of hands, singing in the Spirit, singing of Scripture, spontaneous praise, and applause are acceptable responses to the presence of the Lord—and silly as they seem to some, they are fragrant to God and strengthening to the Body of Christ.

Worship and Warfare

We sometimes think of worship and warfare as being diametrically opposite functions. Instead, they are inextricably entwined in the spirit realm. The battle of Jericho began when Joshua worshiped the Captain of the Lord of hosts the night before the Jericho conquest began. Significantly, the battle ended with Israel's worshipful shout to God.

The battle of Jericho was won with the shout of praise! (See Joshua 6:20.) In Revelation 8, after the angel poured out the incense before the throne, great peals of thunder began, followed by the wrath and judgment of God upon the ungodly.

The call of Jericho is a call to aggressive spiritual warfare. This kind of warfare begins and ends with worship. In our battles against the forces of

> The call of Jericho is a call to aggressive spiritual warfare.

darkness, we dare not rush in where angels fear to tread. Instead, we first come into the presence of our heavenly Captain and worship in the beauty of His holiness. It is in His presence that we receive our directives and strategies. Praise, worship, prayer, and intercession are our spiritual weapons. Psalm 149:6-9 says:

> *Let the high praises of God be in their mouth, and a*
> *two-edged sword* [the Word] *in their hand, to execute*
> *vengeance on the nations and punishment on the peoples,*
> *to bind their kings with chains and their nobles with*
> *fetters of iron, to execute on them the judgment written;*
> *this is an honor for all His godly ones. Praise the Lord!*

What an encouragement to be a people of praise! Praise accomplishes great things in the realm of the Spirit. Praise and prayer are mighty weapons to be used in aggressive conflict with the forces of darkness. Praising people are powerful people. When

> Praise and prayer are mighty weapons to be used in aggressive conflict with the forces of darkness.

we apply these principles of aggressive spiritual warfare, we will give birth to restoration and revival.

Remember, Jesus said the gates of hell would not prevail against the onslaught of the Church (see Matt. 16:18). In Isaiah 53:12 the Spirit of the Lord declares that Christ will divide the spoils of battle among the strong; and in Ephesians 6:10, Paul admonishes us to *"be strong in the Lord."*

Praise is the highest expression of faith we can render to God in the face of spiritual battle. Praise demonstrates reliance, not on one's abilities, but on the incomparable strength of God. I know that, apart from Him, I am no match for the enemy; but praise releases the presence of God. Psalm 97:5 reveals the power of His presence, saying, *"the mountains melted like wax at the presence of the Lord..."*!

As we praise Him in the great congregation, His very presence causes mountains of satanic oppression to be removed. *"Let God arise, let His enemies be scattered..."* cried the psalmist (Ps. 68:1). Jericho—then and now—is a place of absolute victory resulting from surrender, worship, and praise.

Prepare for the New Wine

While these truths have been shared repeatedly by many great men and women of God, there is still more to be learned. The days ahead will be marked by even greater expressions of celebration in His presence—if we are willing to be taught from the Word by the Spirit of the Lord.

As we ask God for "new wine," we must remember that new wineskins will be needed to receive His outpouring. Praise and worship will enable us to function on increasingly supernatural levels. Let's allow God to do a work in our hearts and to enlarge our understanding in the days that lie ahead. In the words of the Bonnie Low song, "For the Lord Is Marching On":

> "For the Lord is marching on
> And His army is ever strong
> And His glory shall be seen upon our land!
> Raise the anthem, sing the victor's song
> Praise the Lord, for the battle's won
> No weapon formed against us shall stand
> For the Captain of the host is Jesus
> We're following in His footsteps.
> No foe can stand against us in the fray
> We are marching in Messiah's band
> The keys of victory in His mighty hand
> Let us march on to take our promised land!"[2]

Endnotes

1. Biblesoft's New Exhaustive Strong's Numbers and Concordance with Expanded Greek-Hebrew Dictionary. CD-ROM. Biblesoft, Inc. and International Bible Translators, Inc. s.v. "Jericho," (OT 3405).

2. Bonnie Low, "For the Lord Is Marching On," published by Scripture in Song (1977), http://www.higherpraise.com/lyrics/love/love853017.htm (accessed March 18, 2009).

POINTS TO PONDER

1. "It is not enough to tithe and be on the membership roles of a local church. It isn't even enough to be present at all the meetings. …[Some people] become permanent but immovable fixtures." Does that describe you? Are you a *permanent but immovable* fixture in the house of God?

2. What is the significance of Jericho and what does it symbolize for us today?

3. Can you think of other examples in the Bible of when praise, worship, and prayer have been used to gain victory over the enemy? Look through the Bible and make a list. Then ask God to help you learn from their examples.

CHAPTER 5

ROLL, JORDAN, ROLL!

The sons of the prophets who were at Jericho approached Elisha and said to him, "Do you know that the Lord will take away your master from over you today?" And he answered, "Yes, I know; be still." Then Elijah said to him, "Please stay here, for the Lord has sent me to the Jordan." And he said, "As the Lord lives, and as you yourself live, I will not leave you." So the two of them went on.
(2 Kings 2:5-6)

Every phase of growth that comes by the Spirit of God causes us to appreciate the steps preceding it. We don't always understand why the Lord leads us in certain pathways; at least not until we see in hindsight where those pathways took us.

Each step we take is built on an earlier foray into the things of God. We have seen the importance of advancing from Gilgal to Bethel and on to Jericho. We have seen how the circumcision of our hearts leads to commitment and accountability; and how commitment and accountability lead us into warfare—not with each other, but with demonic spirits.

At some point in our journey, God calls us eastward to the Jordan. Yet, in the Scriptures, east represents not a destination but the place of beginnings. We know, for instance, that Judah, the leading tribe of Israel, camped at the eastern end of the tabernacle (see Num. 2:3).

So, while we begin our spiritual journey in Gilgal, traveling west to Bethel and east again to Jericho, the Jordan (our journey's end) is farther east than Gilgal, the place of our beginning. The full circle of this spiritual venture is like life itself—it has unexpected yet meaningful twists and turns.

> The full circle of this spiritual venture is like life itself—it has unexpected yet meaningful twists and turns.

Why would God call Elijah to go backward? The answer has to do with humility; in the Kingdom of God, we must sometimes go backward in order to move forward. The road to exaltation always passes through a place called Humility.

Spiritually Fat or Fruitful?

Elisha had clung to Elijah all morning. They began their journey at Gilgal and, probably by mid-morning, arrived at Bethel. After leaving Bethel, they trekked to Jericho. They had walked at least 15 miles. It could well have been late afternoon by then. A dip in the muddy Jordan might have seemed a refreshing and welcome prospect.

Elisha's heart burned for more of what God had for him. Sadly, the sons of the prophets had no empathy for the spiritual depths he desired to explore. Similarly today, some in the Church have made Jericho their home. They are beyond Bethel; they sing, praise, and celebrate the Lord wholeheartedly. They might even dance on occasion. They seem to understand spiritual warfare and appear to have faith that moves mountains. They read the latest Christian books, subscribe to Christian e-mails and magazines, attend conferences, and watch 24-hour Christian programming—yet something is missing from their lives.

What has gone wrong? In the second chapter of Revelation, John wrote a letter on behalf of the Lord Jesus to the church at Ephesus. Within two years of being established, this church had grown to 40,000 members. Their doctrines were correct; their standards were high. Yet Jesus was disappointed with them. Why? Because they left their first love (see Rev. 2:4). They had reduced everything to a set of rules and regulations. Having developed a pattern of Christian "professionalism," they had gone only as far as Bethel. They meant well, but missed the mark.

It would be easy to judge them too harshly; instead, let's examine our own lives. None of us are exempt from the wiles of the enemy. The church at Ephesus had been so well fed that they believed they had "arrived." They failed to distinguish their fattened intellectualism from the fruit of a transformed heart. Is the same thing happening to us?

Not Soft in the Lord, but Strong

Jordan was a consequential point in Elisha's spiritual journey. So it is for the development of the Church. If we are to rise to the

> The message of the cross must not be written only on the tablet of our minds; it must be engraved upon our hearts.

occasion, the message of the cross must not be written only on the tablet of our minds; it must be engraved upon our hearts. Rather than being content to settle into a Christian comfort zone, the cross taken to heart will inspire a state of readiness to enter the fray, an Elisha-like determination to take the next fateful step and contend for the promises and anointing of God.

To contend in this way, we must resist discouragement; therefore, our roots must go deep. Unlike those who chase after the so-called deep things of God, yet remain shallow in understanding and character, we are called to *"prepare* [our] *minds for action, keep sober in spirit, fix* [our] *hope completely on the grace to be brought to* [us] *at the revelation of Jesus Christ"* (1 Pet. 1:13).

In other words, we are to become truth-ready, as Elisha was. There is an old proverb that says: *When the student is ready, the teacher appears.* The transfer—of knowledge or the anointing—can happen only when someone is positioned, as Elisha was, to receive it. Such a student is truth-ready; he or she is prepared and committed to not only receive truth, but to act upon it.

The Charismatic Church is not lacking in truth. The Church has imparted great truths to multitudes worldwide. Unfortunately, many of these truths have not taken root. The circumstance is not new: once upon a time in the wilderness, a man named Moses had a similar problem. Listen to the sermon he preached to the people:

But Jeshurun grew fat and kicked—you are grown fat, thick, and sleek—then he forsook God who made him, and scorned the Rock of his salvation (Deuteronomy 32:15).

Some of us have become spiritual gluttons! Connoisseurs of the finest doctrinal exposition, we sample here and there until our minds are full. Instead of becoming strong, we become soft; instead of developing spiritual muscle, we cultivate fat heads and lean hearts. God declared that this kind of spiritual gluttony led to a scornful attitude in the sons of Israel.

When we grow fat, we kick and complain and scorn the Rock of our salvation. We need to learn how to hunger and thirst after righteousness all over again, with Jesus as our prime example. Do you remember what Jesus said to His "well-fed" disciples? He said, *"I have food to eat that you do not know about"* (John 4:32).

Scripture tells us that strong meat belongs to the mature (see Heb. 5:12,14). Jesus went on to tell His disciples what a diet of strong meat is; He said, *"My food is to do the will of Him who sent Me…"* (John 4:34). Doing the will of the Father is the strong meat of the mature believer!

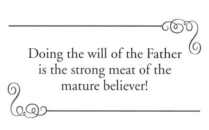

Doing the will of the Father is the strong meat of the mature believer!

Strength Through Maturity

As the season of transition ripens, those who are alert to the signs of the times and steadfast in their commitment to God will be positioned, as Elisha was, for the transfer of the mantle. These modern-day Elishas are spiritually mature and determined to re-sist discouragement. But other qualities mark their lives and em-power them to stand firm over the long haul.

They are a company of believers who are open to experiencing all that God has for them. They don't see their lives as being constricted; for them, tarrying is not the only option. These are the worshiping warriors who become perseverant participants. They summon up the spiritual wherewithal to say, "As the Lord lives, and as long as I am alive on this earth, I will go on to my Jordan with God."

> Today's Elishas have confidence in Him and trust that He is backing them up as they obey His call forward.

They are conscientious, dependable, committed, ded-icated. They operate in self-mastery; they control their thoughts, inclinations, atti-tudes, and choices. They recognize God-created oppor-tunities and are willing to withstand whatever challenges are nec-essary to follow through with God.

Today's Elishas have confidence in Him and trust that He is backing them up as they obey His call forward. They are confi-dent also in the tools God has given them; they know that God has provided the means to achieve His desired ends. And they know they are able to stand up to the devil and win:

> *For the weapons of our warfare are not of the flesh, but divinely powerful for the destruction of fortresses. We are destroying speculations and every lofty thing raised up against the knowledge of God, and we are taking every thought captive to the obedience of Christ* (2 Corinthians 10:4-5).

God's army for this hour will consist of people who will press forward in hope, regardless of the obstacles. They will boldly say: *"By You I can run upon a troop; and by my God I can leap over a wall"* (Ps. 18:29). They will be resilient, able to bounce back from setbacks and overcome enemies because they know the living God who is able to raise even the dead!

Obedience: The Core of Maturity

In the end, maturity is a byproduct of obedience to God. That obedience is the base price of your ticket to Jordan.

Absolute surrender and obedience are what the Word requires of us. In the days ahead, we need to hear the truth of absolute obedience to the Lordship of Jesus Christ again and again. If we want all that God intends for us, we cannot be content to remain at Jericho. We must go on to the Jordan.

Let me warn you—the Jordan is not entirely inviting. In fact, the name *Jordan* means "the descender";[1] it is a picture of death. Yet, the Jordan is where we must go.

Burial "at sea," anyone?

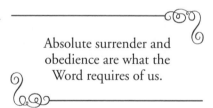

Absolute surrender and obedience are what the Word requires of us.

Endnote

1. Biblesoft's New Exhaustive Strong's Numbers and Concordance with Expanded Greek-Hebrew Dictionary. CD-ROM. Biblesoft, Inc. and International Bible Translators, Inc. s.v. "Jordan" (OT 3383).

POINTS TO PONDER

1. "The transfer [of the anointing] can happen only when someone is positioned, as Elisha was, to receive it. Such a student is truth-ready; he or she is prepared and committed not only to receive truth, but to act upon it." Are you a truth-ready student?

2. "Absolute surrender and obedience are what the Word requires of us." Have you surrendered everything in your life—your plans, possessions, control, *everything*—to God? Are you ready and willing to obey whatever He commands?

CHAPTER 6

CROSSING OVER ON DRY GROUND

*Now fifty men of the sons of the prophets went and stood
opposite them at a distance, while the two of them stood by
the Jordan. Elijah took his mantle and folded it together
and struck the waters, and they were divided here and there,
so that the two of them crossed over on dry ground.*
(2 Kings 2:7-8)

Jordan, the place of descent, is not for the faint of heart. It is a
picture of death and transition.

The Jordan is the one place to which the sons of the prophets
would not tag along. At best, they watched from a distance. They
were content with their ministry status quo; they were happy to
stay behind and "mind the shop." The sons of the prophets were
not participants in God's move; they were spectators.

From Jordan, Elijah would be escorted to Heaven. It was the
place where Elisha would be required to leave behind his ministry
to the man of God and fulfill his new ministry—without his
mentor at his side.

Jordan had long been revered as a site with historical and spiritual significance. Do you remember what happened when the sons of Israel came to the banks of the Jordan in Joshua's day? The people were commanded to follow 2,000 cubits behind the Ark of the Covenant as it was carried by the priests into Jordan's muddy waters (see Josh. 3:4). This symbolized to the people that God, the Way Maker, was going before them to bring them into the Promised Land.

This is consistent with the character and ways of God. He always goes before His people. In this case, the Ark would enter the Jordan (which was at flood stage) before the Israelites did. Because of the presence of the Ark (which symbolizes the fullness of the Godhead), the Jordan parted and the people passed over easily.

Parting the Waters of Death

We know the fullness of the Godhead is contained in the Lord Jesus Christ (see Col. 2:9). When He began His earthly ministry, Jesus entered Jordan's waters to be baptized. This was an important step in the fulfillment of His mission on earth (see Matt. 3:15).

In Jesus' life, baptism was (as it is today) symbolic of death and resurrection. Jesus' act of obedience caused Heaven to open, the Spirit to descend upon Him, and the Father to utter these words: *"You are My beloved Son, in You I am well-pleased"* (Luke 3:22). Jesus' experience at the Jordan was a turning point in His ministry.

Elijah and Elisha also reached a critical juncture at the Jordan; it was for them a point of no return. Once they arrived at Jordan, all other earthly ties and relationships became distant.

Relationally speaking, they had reached their irreducible minimum; apart from God, there were just the two of them—two who walked in agreement together for the plan of the Almighty (see Amos 3:3). They had come to Jordan to seal the deal and see death give way to life.

Jordan's "waters of death" were, in effect, a temporary barrier blocking the transaction. Yet, the two prophets, who represented Israel's former generation and the generation to come, were not to halt at Jordan's banks. They had to cross the river. A significant chapter in divine history would culminate on the other side.

Elijah confronted the obstacle head on; he removed his mantle and rolled it up. Elijah took his coat of cloth and made of it a rod with which to strike the waters. The mantle represents Elijah's anointing, which was adaptable to the situation at hand. The anointing was about to accomplish what was needed at the time.

That rod (or stick) is a type of the cross; it represents the finished work of Christ, the position from which we reckon ourselves dead to sin and alive to God (see Rom. 6:11). It's where we realize that sin no longer dominates our lives. It is the place where we realize that our needs—for peace, healing, provision, and everything else—have been met.

Elijah's was an act of faith much like that of Moses who stretched out his hand over the Red Sea (see Exod. 14:21). Elijah struck the waters with his "rod." The waters of death rolled back, and the two men crossed over on dry ground. Instead of tasting death's waters (as Pharaoh's army had), they were divinely "delivered" to the other side.

The ground across which they walked can also be seen as symbolic. It represents the ground of our being, our "rootedness" in God's love, and the death and burial of Jesus Christ.

From Death to Life

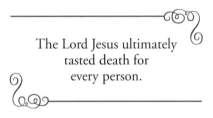

The Lord Jesus ultimately tasted death for every person.

The Lord Jesus ultimately tasted death for every person. He entered into the waters of death, not only symbolically, but literally.

...Although He existed in the form of God, [He] did not regard equality with God a thing to be grasped, but emptied Himself, taking the form of a bond-servant, and being made in the likeness of men. Being found in appearance as a man, He humbled Himself by becoming obedient to the point of death, even death on a cross (Philippians 2:6-8).

From the beginning of His public ministry, Jesus lived the principle revealed in the symbolism of the Jordan: death to self-will. Some would say that Jesus' struggle in the Garden of Gethsemane was a sign that He wavered in His commitment to the cross. But in Matthew chapter 4, we see that Jesus had already made His choice; the struggle in Gethsemane was simply the outworking of His wilderness experience. His meat had always been to do the Father's will, regardless of the cost.

We've seen that Jesus is the fullness of the Godhead and we know His work on the cross stands as a finished work. If all that is true, why isn't the Gilgal experience enough? Why is the journey to Jordan necessary?

Gilgal is transformative; it is where we realize that Christ died *for us.* It is also where we must realize that Christ died *as us.* In other words, when Christ died, we died! He took the punishment we deserved.

> While His work on Calvary has imparted new life and righteousness and freed us from condemnation, living out that new life requires ongoing choices.

But it is only when we arrive at Jordan that we understand the necessity of Christ's death becoming effective *in us!* While His work on Calvary has imparted new life and righteousness and freed us from condemnation, living out that new life requires ongoing choices.

This lifelong process is called *sanctification.* It is accomplished by God's grace, just as salvation is. Grace divinely enables us to fulfill the will of the Father and negate the will of self. Grace is God's power to apply the death of Christ to our everyday lives so that we can be transformed into His image.

Paul prayed for this outcome in Philippians 3:10-11:

> *That I may know Him* [as Elisha knew Him] *and the power of His resurrection and the fellowship of His sufferings* [the Jordan], *being conformed to His death; in order that I may attain to the resurrection from the dead.*

A babe in Christ (one having only the Gilgal revelation) cannot handle the full intent of the cross. Surely he can appreciate that old things are passing away, but becoming new on a practical level takes many choices that are not yet evident at Gilgal.

The repentance that releases salvation is both a single act and a lifetime walk. Young converts are carried and coddled by the Father because they are babes who rightly thrive on milk. But in every species, the young are expected to mature.

> Spiritually speaking, problems arise when those who should be ready for meat refuse to graduate to an adult diet.

Spiritually speaking, problems arise when those who should be ready for meat refuse to graduate to an adult diet. Like the sons of the prophets, they choose to go only so far and no farther. They resist moving forward; instead they hang onto the old ways, beliefs, and sins hidden in their hearts.

Consider this practical illustration to which many of us can relate. I used to have a junk closet where I kept items of sentimental value. Year after year, the collection grew larger. I never used any of these things, but I couldn't bear to part with them. When I got married, I brought the stuff with me. My wife, who had no sentimental attachment to any of it, disposed of it.

Our relationship with Jesus works the same way. We were married to sin before we met Christ; but after we met Him we changed partners. He then began to clean out our spiritual closets. The psalmist explains that God shines His light on our "secret sins" when we come into His presence (see Ps. 90:8).

Embrace the Journey

Without a doubt, we should rejoice in the Gilgal experience and shout, "Hooray! He took my sins away!" Likewise, we should validate our need for the security, fellowship, and caring community provided by the Bethel revelation. Should we then discredit the excitement we feel when we experience victory for the Kingdom? Certainly not! Bringing down our walls of Jericho (enemy strongholds) is a vital part of our Christian walk.

God uses the entire journey to bring us to the Jordan, which is an experience each of us must face alone. It is an intimate place where God gets very personal and particular with us. It is here where He deals the deathblow to those things we secretly value as much as (or more than) we value Him.

Some of these hidden things come packaged in religious boxes. Others are carnal ambitions that run contrary to the nature and character of Christ. Whatever form these distractions take, the Surgeon's knife—the double-edged sword of His Word—will be unsheathed at Jordan to slice through them:

> *For the word of God is living and active and sharper than any two-edged sword, and piercing as far as the division of soul and spirit, of both joints and marrow, and able to judge the thoughts and intentions of the heart* (Hebrews 4:12).

God will use the Jordan experience to expose our motives, dismantle our schemes, and cause us to relinquish our insistence on having things our way.

How often do we ask for a deeper walk with God, praying, "God, do a deep work in me. I want to be used mightily of You. I want the supernatural to be manifested in my life"? God then takes us at our word and gives us what we ask for. Unfortunately, we don't recognize it when it comes, because we really didn't understand what we were asking for!

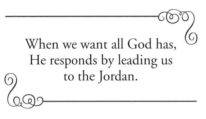

When we want all God has, He responds by leading us to the Jordan.

When we want all God has, He responds by leading us to the Jordan. What happens next isn't all that pretty. Instead of being immediately gratified, promoted, or recognized by others, we find God exposing our so-called good works (the ones driven by impure motives) for what they are. Instead of polishing our shiny exteriors, we find our sin being uncovered at its very roots.

The Jordan will cost us everything. Paul explained it this way: *"Do you not know that all of us who have been baptized into Christ Jesus have been baptized into His death?"* (Rom. 6:3). Many have been overwhelmed and overjoyed by the baptism and gifts of the Holy Spirit, but these are only a doorway into Jordan. In the decades since the Charismatic Renewal began, multitudes have had the Pentecostal experience; yet, too many have sought the power without desiring a deep relationship with the Person.

The Person is the power! You can't have the gifts without the Giver of the gifts—the Person of the Holy Spirit. Furthermore, He is holy; and until we emphasize holiness as He does, our quest for the gifts will be hollow and fueled by wrong desires.

When John the Baptist spoke of Jesus' ministry, he declared: *"As for me, I baptize you with water for repentance, but He who is coming after me is mightier than I…He will baptize you with the Holy Spirit and fire"* (Matt. 3:11). When we receive the Holy Spirit, we get the fire that comes with Him. You can't have one without the other.

The Person is the power!

Divine Life—By Fire

Isaiah asked the following question about our ability to handle fire: *"…Who among us can live with the consuming fire? Who among us can live with continual burning?"* (Isa. 33:14).

If we assume these verses refer only to the fires of hell, we miss their relevance for the present day. To live in God's presence is to live in the fire. He baptizes us with fire; it facilitates the perfecting of the image of Christ in us by consuming dross and yielding pure gold (the image of Christ).

As we come face to face with God and behold Him in all His glory, the fire of His presence stirs up the impurities in our hearts (the dross) and brings them to the surface. As we cooperate with Him, the impurities are skimmed off. Paul puts it this way:

> *But we all, with unveiled face, beholding as in a mirror the glory of the Lord, are being transformed into the same image from glory to glory, just as from the Lord, the Spirit* (2 Corinthians 3:18).

This is the message of the Jordan. I believe with all my heart that the days ahead will be marked by a return to the apostolic preaching of the cross. God is calling us more than ever in this hour to come to the Jordan. There is new life to be gained in the waters of death.

Let's further explore our relationship with fire and see how Isaiah describes those who can live in the fire:

> *"...Who among us can live with the consuming fire?..."*
> *He who walks righteously and speaks with sincerity, he who rejects unjust gain and shakes his hands so that they hold no bribe; he who stops his ears from hearing about bloodshed and shuts his eyes from looking upon evil; he will dwell on the heights, his refuge will be the impregnable rock; his bread will be given him, his water will be sure* (Isaiah 33:14-16).

Fire is the agent of God that purifies our character. The more we cooperate, the more precious gold and silver will be revealed and the greater the power of God that will be released through us.

This process is necessary both individually and corporately. As we learn to respond appropriately to the fire of God, it becomes the light in our hearts that burns brighter and brighter, yielding the godly zeal that drives the Church to new heights of glory!

> Fire is the agent of God that purifies our character.

We need to be able to say with Christ that *"zeal for Your house [consumes] Me"* (Ps. 69:9; John 2:17). It is time to cast off the fear of change. Rather than stand at a distance from Jordan, let's advance to its banks with Elisha and allow God to move in all His fullness in and

It is time to cast off the fear of change.

through our lives. Let's become the fulfillment of the words David prophesied long ago: *"Your people will volunteer freely in the day of Your power..."* (Ps. 110:3).

Willingness will cause the waters to part, and we will cross over Jordan on dry ground. So, arise, let us go from here!

POINTS TO PONDER

1. "God uses the entire journey to bring us to the Jordan, which is an experience each of us must face alone. It is an intimate place where God gets very personal and particular with us. It is here where He deals the deathblow to those things we secretly value as much as (or more than) we value Him." Take a minute and be honest with yourself and with God. What is it that you value the most?

2. "Many have sought the power without desiring a deep relationship with the Person. The Person *is* the power! You can't have the gifts without the Giver of the gifts—the Person of the Holy Spirit." Are you fascinated by and hungry for the power and excitement of the *gifts* of the Spirit? Are you even *more* thrilled to know God Himself? Where is your focus and love: on the gifts or on the Giver?

CHAPTER 7

WHAT DO YOU WANT?

When they had crossed over, Elijah said to Elisha, "Ask
what I shall do for you before I am taken from you." And
Elisha said, "Please, let a double portion of your spirit be
upon me." He said, "You have asked a hard thing.
Nevertheless, if you see me when I am taken from you, it
shall be so for you; but if not, it shall not be so."
(2 Kings 2:9-10)

When a man and woman are serious about their romantic relationship, they can't see enough of each other. They become inseparable.

At some point, the woman begins to anticipate the moment
when her Prince Charming will pop the question. She rehearses
her answer, eager for the day to come. On a certain day, the moment arrives; her dream becomes reality and the bride-to-be is
ready for it.

Elisha was ready, too. He knew what he wanted. His heart was
prepared for the realization of his dream. Some of us never receive
answers to our prayers, either because we're afraid to ask or

because we're not sure what we want. Not Elisha! He knew exactly what he wanted and was determined to receive it.

Ask, Seek, Knock

Consider for a moment what had transpired to this point: Elisha had clung relentlessly to Elijah even when Elijah seemed to give him the brush-off. It seems clear that Elijah was not upset with his disciple's tenacity; God had already shown Elijah His plans for the protégé.

Hearing from God was important, but Elijah needed to hear from Elisha, too. The up-and-coming prophet would have to say what he wanted, not because his predecessor needed information, but because the vision needed to be verbalized by Elisha. Why? Because unless we verbalize our desires,

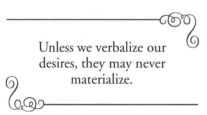

Unless we verbalize our desires, they may never materialize.

they may never materialize. Jesus said that we could have whatever we say, not whatever we *think* (see Mark 11:23).

Elisha's words and actions to that point revealed much of what was in his heart. Elijah had seen his protégé's tenacity. Through all of the testing he had endured, Elisha's speech never changed. His response was always the same: *"As the Lord lives, and as you yourself live, I will not leave you"* (2 Kings 2:2,4,6).

There was a shared history between these two men. God had directed Elijah to Elisha, but there was something more to the equation. There had to have been something in Elisha—a desire for what Elijah had—that brought God to his doorstep, so to speak. Elisha's desire was evident to God *before* Elijah threw his mantle upon him (see 1 Kings 19:19). This desire caused Elisha to cleave to Elijah; it also kept Elijah at his protégé's side.

Elisha's resolve never diminished. His faith remained steadfast, and his intentions remained clear. Nothing but death would separate him from Elijah. I can imagine Elijah's thoughts about his protégé: *You didn't allow me to leave you at Gilgal. You stuck to me like glue when I tried to move on from Bethel without you. And even at Jericho, you refused to be shaken off. I know what God told me about you, and I can see how determined you are to receive it.*

The relationship had reached critical mass. Now something was needed to ignite the transaction. Elijah knew just what to do: he brought an irresistible force—a simple, powerful question—to bear on Elisha's immovable intent. Elijah's question focused Elisha's vision with a few blunt words: "Elisha, what do you want?"

Elisha was poised for the moment. Like the young woman awaiting a proposal from her beloved, he had his answer in mind and unloaded it without hesitation. His words revealed an awareness of his calling: "I want a double portion of your spirit…the holy breath that resides in you. Bequeath me your spirit."

> Elijah's question focused Elisha's vision with a few blunt words: "Elisha, what do you want?"

Elijah's question seized Elisha at his core and launched him on the balance of his quest. His response defined his desire and clarified what he didn't want. Elisha was not after anything he could see. He was not interested in inheriting Elijah's reputation. He cared nothing for his mentor's coat. What he wanted was the spirit that caused Ahab and Jezebel to fear Elijah—the same spirit that could bring dead boys back to life.

But there was something more to what Elisha was asking of Elijah. His request went beyond the substance of the anointing, to the matter of an inheritance. Consider Deuteronomy 21:17:

> *But he shall acknowledge the firstborn…by giving him a double portion of all that he has, for he is the beginning of his strength; to him belongs the right of the firstborn.*

Elisha wanted the rights of the firstborn son! Elijah had no sons, at least none that we know of. Nevertheless, Elisha was his son in the faith, much as Timothy was Paul's spiritual son. The firstborn "owns" the birthright and receives the inheritance.

Spiritually speaking, the ultimate fulfillment of the rights of the firstborn is found in Jesus Christ. Hebrews 1:6, 8-9 explains:

> *And when He again brings the firstborn into the world, He says, "And let all the angels of God worship Him."…But of the Son He says, "Your throne, O God, is forever and ever, and the righteous scepter is the scepter of His kingdom. You have loved righteousness and hated lawlessness; therefore God, Your God, has anointed You with the oil of gladness **above** Your companions."*

Jesus Christ has preeminence over all the works of God's hands. He is our Elder Brother and sovereign Lord. What Elisha was asking for was the right to inherit all that Elijah had. This was a spiritual inheritance. The double portion was the very authority and prophetic mantle in which Elijah walked.

Preparing for Transfer

Elisha made quite a request! In reality, it was not Elijah who had the power to bequeath his spirit, but God, who had already mapped out the process. Was God put off by Elisha's big ideas? Absolutely not! God approves of big dreams. He places them in our hearts and then specializes in doing the impossible.

> God approves of big dreams. He places them in our hearts and then specializes in doing the impossible.

Why, then, did Elijah say that Elisha asked "a hard thing"? There were a number of reasons. First, Elijah understood that Elisha's ministry would be a ministry of seeing. It would begin with his ability to stay focused on his master. Elijah said:

> *You have asked a hard thing. Nevertheless, **if you see me when I am taken from you,** it shall be so for you; but if not, it shall not be so* (2 Kings 2:10).

Elijah knew that without spiritual sight into the invisible realm, Elisha could not and would not obtain what he desired. If Elisha meant business, he would have to know exactly what he wanted and he would have to see and understand what God was doing. (We'll see later how Elisha passed this "vision" test.)

Like Elisha in his day, we must determine what we want from God in this era. Now that the Charismatic tide has ebbed and flowed through various seasons, are we going to believe for greater things or cede our spiritual territory over to the devil and wait passively for the Rapture to come?

I believe God has more—much more! And I believe He wants us to ask Him for it; we are to ask, seek, and knock (see Matt. 7:7). We need to believe God for an outpouring of the Spirit that will outshine anything we have experienced so far. We need to believe for greater victory!

Those who dwell in darkness are convinced that doom is coming. Global terrorism, economic certainty, and other disasters are very real threats. Should we (the Church), the light of the world and the salt of the earth, be preaching pessimism? No! We are to proclaim the answer—Christ, the very hope of glory!

Everything that Christ has is available to the Church.

Instead of consigning the planet to the antichrist and the hosts of hell, we should be storming Heaven for a rain of glory. The prophet of old said, "Ask for rain in the time of the latter rain" (see Zech. 10:1). In essence, Zechariah was saying, "Don't ask for a drizzle; ask for a downpour!"

Everything that Christ has is available to the Church. The double portion is available to the many sons and daughters born of the Son. I believe the Lord is giving the Church an invitation in this hour. It is the same one Elijah gave Elisha: "Ask what I shall do for you."

Our response can turn the tide of history!

Points to Ponder

1. "Elijah's question focused Elisha's vision with a few blunt words: 'Elisha, what do you want?'" If someone asked *you* that question, what would your answer be?

2. "Everything that Christ has is available to the Church." Make a list of all that Christ has and then ask God how *you* can be a part of making it (and Him) more evident in the Church.

CHAPTER 8

HAVE A SINGLE EYE

As they were going along and talking, behold, there
appeared a chariot of fire and horses of fire which separated
the two of them. And Elijah went up by a whirlwind to
heaven. Elisha saw it and cried out, "My father, my father,
the chariots of Israel and its horsemen!" And he saw Elijah
no more....
(2 Kings 2:11-12)

Nothing worth having comes easy. The God-given desires we harbor in our hearts will be fulfilled, but at a cost. The price is worth paying.

Elijah put a condition on Elisha's request: *"If you see me when I go, you'll receive the double portion"* (see 2 Kings 2:10). It wasn't enough for Elisha to cling to his master from city to city; he had to keep his eyes fixed on Elijah and never let him out of his sight!

This singleness of eye is a rare commodity, even in the Body of Christ. Jesus said the lamp of the body is the eye (see Matt. 6:22). Spiritually speaking, when the eye is single (clear), the whole being is bathed in light. Conversely, when the eye is not single (*i.e.,* the heart is divided), the whole person is darkened (see Matt. 6:23).

Paul exhorted the believers at Colossae to *"set* [their minds] *on the things above"* (Col. 3:2). If our faith is to be perfected, we are to look at Jesus and fix our gaze upon Him (see Heb. 12:2). Just as Elisha fixed his eyes on Elijah in order to receive the double portion, we must rivet our eyes to the One from whom *our* spiritual inheritance flows!

Some have placed their faith in the teachings, methods, or precepts of people; but true faith is rightly fastened to the Lord Jesus Christ, who is the *"head over all things to the church"* (Eph 1:22). Any other placement of our trust is in error. Yes. Church growth principles are good and have their place, but outward success doesn't necessarily imply the genuine touch of God. We need to have the singleness of purpose that the Godhead shares if we are to see God's best in the Church.

> We need to have the singleness of purpose that the Godhead shares if we are to see God's best in the Church.

In Ephesians 1:9-10, Paul reveals the ultimate intention of the Father's eternal purposes:

> *He made known to us the mystery of His will, according to His kind intention which He purposed in Him with **a view to an administration suitable to the fullness of the times, that is, the summing up of all things in Christ,** things in the heavens and things on the earth....*

God has His eyes on one thing: the summing up of all things in Christ, who is to be the center of all our activities, the crowning glory of the Church. If we are to receive a double portion as Elisha did, our eyes need to be directed toward Christ. There is one will in Heaven. There should be one will on earth, too.

> If we are to receive a double portion as Elisha did, our eyes need to be directed toward Christ. There is one will in Heaven. There should be one will on earth, too.

Eyes and Ears for God

The eye mirrors the spirit. If our eyes are not single and intent on one purpose, then our hearts are divided. James had a strong warning for the early Church in this regard:

> *Draw near to God and He will draw near to you. Cleanse your hands, you sinners; and purify your hearts, you **double-minded*** (James 4:8).

God is looking for a modern-day company of men and women who will walk with Him and carry His glory into their family dealings, their workplaces, and their endeavors. This will be a company of believers determined to protect and carry forward the inheritance of God.

We need to keep our eyes on what the Lord is doing and follow Him. We also need to listen for His voice. Two recurring phrases that the Lord Jesus used in the Gospels and in the Book of Revelation are: "He who has ears to hear…" and "He who has an ear, let him hear what the Spirit says to the churches."

In an age of cascading distractions—mass entertainment, emerging media, ever-advancing technologies, and shifting social structures—it is easy for our time and attention to be consumed unwisely. Our most important preoccupation should be to sit at Jesus' feet.

This is one of the reasons Elijah said to Elisha *"...You have asked a hard thing"* (2 Kings 2:10). Elijah understood man's capacity for distraction. Though he knew Elisha was called, he also recognized what was at stake in the coming "executive transfer." Elijah's departure and replacement would affect Israel long term.

Elisha's "single eye" had to be a prerequisite for his receiving the mantle. Elijah knew that regardless of our callings, if we fail to actively focus on God and listen for His voice, we can wander aimlessly for weeks, even years at a time, relying on our own power and never evaluating the quality of our walk with God. In doing so, we (and those for whom we are responsible) are at a loss, because man's power cannot compare to the power of the Lord.

> Regardless of our callings, if we fail to actively focus on God and listen for His voice, we can wander aimlessly for weeks, even years at a time, relying on our own power and never evaluating the quality of our walk with God.

We need to continually seek Him. Consider the following promise, which is as valid as the day God spoke it to Jeremiah:

> *Thus says the Lord who made the earth, the Lord who formed it to establish it, the Lord is His name, "Call to Me, and I will answer you, and I will tell you great and mighty things, which you do not know"* (Jeremiah 33:2-3).

Chapter 33 of Jeremiah is a promise of revival and restoration! It was a promise with a condition: We are to ask and He will tell us great and mighty things.

Relationship, Perceiving, and Receiving

We don't ask things of strangers; asking God implies relationship. At the moment when Elijah was carried to Heaven in the whirlwind, he and Elisha were immersed in fellowship. Because of their relationship, Elisha was privileged to witness his master's departure.

Elijah's remarkable conveyance to Heaven demonstrated the depth of his relationship with God. Only one other man in the Old Testament had simply "disappeared" into Heaven; it was Enoch, whom the Scriptures say *"walked with God"* (Gen. 5:24).

> Elijah's remarkable conveyance to Heaven demonstrated the depth of his relationship with God.

The relationship between Elijah and Elisha had been formed with this moment in mind; now it was about to end. After they crossed the Jordan, they were separated by *"a chariot of fire and horses of fire"* (2 Kings 2:11). One moment, Elijah was walking beside Elisha (the only other person in the vicinity). The next moment, the whirlwind took him up—and Elisha saw the whole thing.

Elisha accomplished the "hard thing": He perceived and understood the method of Elijah's transport to Heaven, his chariot to the throne, if you will. He demonstrated the spiritual vision and ability to see into the invisible realm. Elijah knew his protégé would need that perception to step into his master's shoes.

But what exactly did Elisha perceive besides the spectacular glory cloud and chariots of God? He perceived the means by which God carried out and executed His plan of succession. He witnessed Elijah's move to the next level and was permitted to see into the realm of God's moving...the storehouse of His glory...the world of our inheritance. He saw into the invisible realm and it changed him forever. Elisha saw what few understand or even know exists—and it qualified him to receive the double portion.

Do you remember the cherubim or *"four living beings"* described in the first chapter of Ezekiel? They gleamed like *"burnished bronze"* (Ezek. 1:5,7). Each had four faces (see Ezek. 1:6,10). These are the four faces of Christ: the face of a man (tempted as all men are tempted), a lion (the King of kings), an ox or bull (representing a servant), and an eagle (the Son of God who soars above all things).

Each cherub also had four wings (see Ezek. 1:6), and a wheel that looked like beryl. The wheels moved with the cherubim (see Ezek. 1:15-16). There was also fire and lightning flashing in the midst of the cherubim (see Ezek. 1:13). These cherubim are the horsemen Elisha saw in Second Kings 2:12. They represent the ways in which God moves in the earth.

Above the chariot that carried Elijah to Heaven was a throne occupied by the Son of Man who snatched Elijah Heavenward. This was the means by which Elijah entered the spirit realm and bypassed death.

Imagine—Elisha saw it all!

My Father, My Father!

Elisha's ability to perceive the unfolding of God's will was proven at the Jordan. His eye was single. He had trained himself to be ready for this monumental event and none of its spiritual significance went unnoticed by him.

Elisha had known that his master was about to be taken away. Yet, in those intense moments of Elijah's "rapture"—in the split second during which their conversation was interrupted by the whirlwind, the chariot, and the horsemen—Elisha's emotions registered the impact of his master's departure.

Elisha was painfully aware of the consequences, not only for him, but for Israel. Hence, he cried out *"My father, my father, the chariots of Israel and its horsemen!"* (2 Kings 2:12). He saw the horsemen and the purposes of God; he witnessed (and was part of) God's method of executive succession. Yet he cried out in grief. He knew that Israel had lost its great protector, the one who was responsible for slaughtering the false prophets of Baal and causing the likes of Ahab and Jezebel to tremble with fear. The nation had lost a prophet who represented strength against domestic and foreign foes. (Elisha's grief is discussed further in the next chapter.)

Elisha was about to receive what his heart longed for: the double portion. Yet, his answered prayer had come at great cost.

Stay Close to God's Move

In the next chapter, we will see that the sons of the prophets, who were probably waiting some distance away, offered to go and look for Elijah (see 2 Kings 2:16). These men may have witnessed the miracle, but from the opposite bank of the Jordan. They did not share or understand the experience. They did not understand what God was doing and were out of the spiritual "flow."

David speaks in Psalm 103:7 of God's choices in revealing Himself: *"He made known His ways to Moses, His **acts** to the sons of Israel."* Not everyone who witnesses a miracle understands God's ways. The sons of Israel saw many signs and wonders in the wilderness, but their hearts were dull and their eyes dim. They grumbled and died without reaching the Promised Land.

> Not everyone who witnesses a miracle understands God's ways.

Moses, however, learned to walk in fellowship with God in the desert; he learned the ways of God, as had Elijah and Elisha. The sons of the prophets, however, were like the doubting sons of Israel; they saw God's acts but failed to understand their significance.

Today, multitudes flock to see miracles. They want to watch someone perform a feat of power in the name of the Lord. But those who are used of God in the working of miracles find themselves stripped of the excitement of miraculous things; they are driven instead by the desire to please God.

Somewhere beyond the Jordan experience, contemporary Elishas are learning the ways of the Lord in the wilderness. They may appear to be doing very little, but they have been allowing God to invest grace in their lives. They are learning to be adaptable and pliable in the hand of the Lord!

The hour is coming when these seemingly obscure people will emerge in God's brilliance. It will happen all over the world. These are the ones who are staying close to the moving of God and the leading of His Spirit, even when it seems as though the "excitement" is wearing off.

They are just like Elisha.

POINTS TO PONDER

1. "In an age of cascading distractions—mass entertainment, emerging media, ever-advancing technologies, and shifting social structures—it is easy for our time and attention to be consumed unwisely. Our most important preoccupation should be to sit at Jesus' feet." Take a few minutes and write down a sample schedule of how you spend a typical day. Or better yet, to get a more accurate look, keep a journal for a few days (or a week) and log where you are and what you're doing. Then add up the hours spent doing activities such as watching television, surfing the Web, and shopping, and compare that to the time you spend sitting at Jesus' feet.

2. What was the price Elisha had to pay in order to receive the answer to his request?

CHAPTER 9

GRIEF BEFORE GROWTH

*...Then he took hold of his own clothes and tore them in
two pieces. He also took up the mantle of Elijah that fell
from him and returned and stood by the bank of the Jordan.
He took the mantle of Elijah that fell from him and struck
the waters and said, "Where is the Lord, the God of Elijah?"
And when he also had struck the waters, they were divided
here and there; and Elisha crossed over.*
(2 Kings 2:12-14)

The sons of the prophets watched from a distance as Elijah was
taken and Elisha reacted to the loss. You'll recall that he cried,
"My father, my father!" Then Elisha tore his clothes to further
demonstrate his grief.

Those who are at a distance cannot appreciate loss until it
touches them personally. How empty the sons of the prophets
were! Many believers today are equally empty. They are not
touched by the hurts or needs of others. They know nothing of
the compassion of Christ or its cost.

Remember the story of the Greeks who wanted to see Jesus? They had heard about His miracles and His ministry and came to the disciples saying, *"We wish to see Jesus"* (John 12:21). Do people want to see Jesus today? Isaiah said Jesus had *"no stately form or majesty"* that we should be attracted to Him (Isa. 53:2). But for those who seek Him, He has this incomparable and sobering message:

> *...unless a grain of wheat falls into the earth and dies, it remains alone; but if it dies, it bears much fruit. He who loves his life loses it, and he who hates his life in this world will keep it to life eternal. If anyone serves Me, he must follow Me; and where I am, there My servant will be also; if anyone serves Me, the Father will honor him* (John 12:24-26).

> Elisha suffered loss, but it was for the purpose of growth!

Elisha suffered loss, but it was for the purpose of growth! As searing as his grief was, it produced fruit in keeping with God's plan. Remember: New wine belongs in new wineskins (see Matt. 9:17). Had Elisha not torn his clothes, he could not have taken on Elijah's mantle.

Unexpected Answers to Prayer

At the flashpoint of his grief, Elisha seemed to have forgotten that he was getting exactly what he'd asked of Elijah. In the midst of great turmoil, his request for the double portion was being satisfied.

Elijah's mantle, the sign of the transaction both men knew was coming, had fallen to the ground. This was the coat Elisha had groomed that very morning. He was the one who made sure it was kept coated with resin and free of flies and other insects. In the end, Elisha had preserved the mantle for himself.

It is strange and wonderful how God works in our lives. We desperately want Him to fulfill the desires of our hearts, yet we are often mystified by the ways in which He actually answers our prayers.

> God doesn't just answer our prayers; He also does a work in our lives that gives the answered prayers new meaning.

God doesn't just answer our prayers; He also does a work in our lives that gives the answered prayers new meaning.

God uses the very prayers we pray to shape us into the design He intended for us.

Anointing, Glory, Stewardship, and Succession

Imagine Elisha's moment of truth. The mantle had just floated to the ground. The two men had journeyed to that spot with a common goal in mind. They walked and talked side by side until those final moments when Elijah was taken.

Elisha had crossed a spiritual threshold; his service to Elijah was over and his ministry was changing. He had served his master faithfully; but now it was time for him to carry the legacy forward. It was time for Elisha to fill Elijah's shoes and advance even further than his master had.

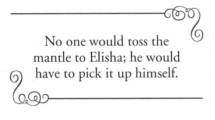

No one would toss the mantle to Elisha; he would have to pick it up himself.

The mantle lying on the ground represented the office for which Elisha had been groomed and the anointing in which Elijah had operated. It pointed to the power that God had invested in His servant and was symbolic of God's glory. This special coat signified the measure of God's Spirit and the stewardship involved for those who answer the call. It was a physical marker of Elisha's appointment to succeed Elijah.

This same coat had already demonstrated the adaptability of the anointing. It was the instrument Elijah used to strike the waters—the method by which the two men crossed the Jordan together. Now the coat was to be taken up by Elijah's successor. This time, no one would toss the mantle to Elisha; he would have to pick it up himself.

Elisha's own clothes, the "uniform" that identified him as Elijah's servant, were torn beyond repair; he could wear them no longer. Under Elijah's mentorship, he had been well prepared. All that time, Elisha had been growing into the mantle of his master. Now it was time to slip into it.

The Cycle of Grief

The irony of Elisha's situation speaks powerfully to our own lives: grief, appropriately processed, is productive.

Grief is not a single emotion, but a cycle of experience. Following Elisha's loss, he was *displaced.* The status quo—his fruitful, nurturing relationship with Elijah—was no more. The time of preparation had come to an abrupt halt. In a moment's time, Elisha had lost his leader and come face to face with the broader implications of his loss.

Elisha's displacement was followed by the sense of being misplaced. Suddenly, that for which he had prayed and been chosen seemed unattractive. The privilege of receiving the double portion of the spirit that had made kings, queens, and priests fearful was not at that moment cause for joy or enthusiasm. The hoped-for outcome had other, less desirable implications.

Still, the wheels of succession had been set in motion; the outcome was irreversible. In spite of his emotions, Elisha would move from the sense of misplacement to the realization that he was most assuredly the replacement God had ordained him to be.

Grief, which we associate with death, is by design a productive cycle. It is emblematic of a genuine ending. It brings closure and the impetus to move forward

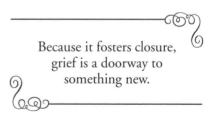

Because it fosters closure, grief is a doorway to something new.

into the next season, a new calling, a new purpose. Because it fosters closure, grief is a doorway to something new. For Elisha and for Israel that was a new focus, a new ministry, and a new era.

Who's Striking the Waters Now?

In Second Kings 2:13, Elisha picked up the fallen mantle and walked back to the bank of the Jordan. Having been a devoted student of Elijah, he well remembered how his master had used the mantle to make passage across the river possible.

Elisha followed his mentor's pattern and struck the waters, but nothing happened. Referring back to Elijah's earlier miracle of parting the waters, Elisha asked: *"Where is the Lord, the God of Elijah?"* In other words, "I've done what my master did and it didn't work!"

The Hebrew indicates that Elisha struck the waters a second time. This time, the waters were divided, and Elisha crossed back over the Jordan, once again crossing over on dry ground.

Why was it necessary for Elisha to strike the waters twice? The process Elisha underwent completed the transfer of the mantle: The first time he used it, he was relying on the God of Elijah, as though his mentor were still there, and Elisha was still his servant.

But Elijah was gone, and Elisha was anointed in his place, serving the God of *Elisha!* Instead of asking the river where God was, he did as his former master had done—he struck the waters, convinced of his authority to do so, and the waters of death backed up.

The transfer was consummated—with witnesses to confirm it. Not only did the Jordan recognize him and obey, but also the sons of the prophets, watching on the opposite bank, now knew that Elisha had inherited the anointing of his mentor.

Beware the Voices of Distraction

The sons of the prophets had seen many manifestations of God's glory during their years of service to Elijah. Yet they were spiritually dull. Instead of encouraging Elisha while Elijah was alive, they served to discourage him (see 2 Kings 2:3,5); instead of wanting to be involved in the move of God, they chose to remain out of reach (see 2 Kings 2:7).

The sons of the prophets asked seemingly logical questions of Elisha; so, while their words were accurate (Elijah *was* going to be taken away that day), their reasons for asking were suspect. They were not trying to inform Elisha (he already knew what was coming); they were testing whether they could distract him enough to set him back from his objective.

Theirs were the voices of petty annoyance, the "little foxes" that ruin the vineyard (see Song of Sol. 2:15). But Elisha's face was set like flint; he recognized their motives and denied them the power to affect him.

Despite their bad intentions, Elisha remained patient with the sons of the prophets, as we'll see in the next chapter. While he remained firm in his own convictions, he allowed these men three days to satisfy their misdirected compulsion to search for Elijah (see 2 Kings 2:16-18).

A Single-Eyed Church

God is equally patient with us. Still, as we approach this season of transition, it is incumbent upon us to resist the voices of distraction and discouragement that have infiltrated the Church over the centuries.

During various Charismatic outpourings, certain churches experienced the clear blessing and presence of the Lord. Healings, miracles, spontaneous praise, and gifts of the Spirit abounded. But many of those who experienced tremendous blessing began to experience a tremendous shaking, too. When they least expected it, great upheaval occurred. Why? Because churches fell asleep.

Often, when God is moving in one area, we assume He is pleased with all the other areas of our lives. This is an unsafe assumption. The same is true for churches. Churches can experience great outpourings, and they begin to expect God to move in certain ways. Even during and after great outpourings, they try to box Him in with rules, regulations, and by-laws that become their gods. In this way, many churches have seen the anointing lift.

> Too many churches that once experienced the glory of the Lord are now empty shells.

Too many churches that once experienced the glory of the Lord are now empty shells. Convinced of their own righteousness, they condemned the very moving of God in their midst. We need to humble ourselves and ask the question the disciples asked Jesus on the night He disclosed His coming betrayal: *"Surely not I?"* (Mark 14:19).

Betrayal is a strong word, but perhaps an appropriate one. While none of us would ever admit to having created barriers against the move of God or advocating a church split, have we, by our attitudes and subjective expectations unwittingly contributed to the waning of our churches? Are we so sold out to our own traditions that we have immunized others against calling a church "home"? Have we backed away from, or encouraged others to back away from, God's presence?

We have to learn to keep the "main thing" the main thing. Churches vary; the One we worship does not. It's time to embrace the differences from church to church: different faces, cultures, worship styles, and any other biblically-sound features that may be new to our way of thinking. The important thing is to be unified in strengthening the Church.

> Churches vary; the One we worship does not.

Let's also be careful not to resent changes or challenges experienced in our churches. Let's learn a lesson from Elisha. Surely he grieved; Elijah was gone and Elisha's life was irrevocably changed. He could not go back to "the way it used to be." There came a time, however, for Elisha to stop grieving and begin to move forward in God's plan.

We need to do the same. You may be in a church right now that hasn't tasted half of what you've experienced in the past. You may feel isolated and alone. Don't rebel against the leadership; don't grumble and complain. Don't look back. God has allowed you to taste something great and glorious. You haven't lost that! It's all there inside you, waiting to explode!

Go back and stand by the banks of the Jordan. Take up the mantle that has fallen from Elijah, the mantle with which he struck the waters. Remember that it symbolizes the finished work of Christ, the truth that we are dead to sin and alive to God (see Rom. 6:11). We needn't be distracted or dominated by sin any longer. Jesus condemned sin in the flesh and proclaimed, *"It is finished"* (John 19:30).

> Those who stand at a distance from the Jordan can never experience the fullness of God's grace, but those who are willing to fellowship with Christ in His sufferings will enter into resurrection life!

Those who stand at a distance from the Jordan can never experience the fullness of God's grace, but those who are willing to fellowship with Christ in His sufferings will enter into resurrection life! It is not until we stand on resurrection ground that we can ask what we will of the Father and have it done for us (see John 15:7).

Elijah was gone, but, for Elisha, the best was yet to come! Assume your rightful place on the Jordan. Stop waiting for God to move through someone else. Lay hold of that for which you were apprehended by Christ Jesus (see Phil. 3:12) and begin to pour out your heart to God. Cast all your cares upon Him (see 1 Pet. 5:7).

Have faith in God, knowing that He who parted the Jordan's waters in the past will part them again. Don't wait for the next move of God; begin moving yourself. Strike the waters as Elisha did (see 2 Kings 2:14) and go forward.

If we will dare in this hour to take the mantle of delegated Kingdom authority and in the name of the Lord Jesus Christ strike the waters of apathy, resistance, and unbelief (the waters of fear and satanic strongholds that hinder God's Spirit), we will find that the God of Elijah will move on our behalf, making a way where there is no way.

He will cause the waters to part and we will cross over on dry ground!

POINTS TO PONDER

1. "The irony of Elisha's situation speaks powerfully to our own lives: grief, appropriately processed, is productive." Consider a time in your own life when you experienced grief. Did you actively work through it and process it? What did you learn through the experience?

2. "While none of us would ever admit to having created barriers against the move of God or advocating a church split, have we, by our attitudes and subjective expectations unwittingly contributed to the waning of our churches? Are we so sold out to our own traditions that we have immunized others against calling a church 'home'? Have we backed away from, or encouraged others to back away from, God's presence?" If so, how?

CHAPTER 10

LOVE RELEASES...FEAR POSSESSES

*Now when the sons of the prophets who were at Jericho opposite
him saw him, they said, "The spirit of Elijah rests on Elisha."
And they came to meet him and bowed themselves to the
ground before him. They said to him, "Behold now, there are
with your servants fifty strong men, please let them go and
search for your master; perhaps the Spirit of the Lord has taken
him up and cast him on some mountain or into some valley."
And he said, "You shall not send." But when they urged him
until he was ashamed, he said, "Send." They sent therefore fifty
men; and they searched three days but did not find him. They
returned to him while he was staying at Jericho; and he said to
them, "Did I not say to you, 'Do not go'?"*
(2 Kings 2:15-18)

Do you long to be used of God in ministry? Have you hungered
in your heart to be His hand extended? Have you ever considered
the struggles of those in ministry? It isn't always glorious, though
some of us would like to think so. (If we see ministry that way,
God will eventually "burst our bubble" for our own good.)

After crossing the Jordan, Elisha was forever changed. He inherited the sons of the prophets, who had not experienced the far side of Jordan as he had. They were void of spiritual insight, as their statements and actions showed.

Elijah was now gone, and Elisha was fulfilling the call of God. Although the sons of the prophets admitted that Elisha was operating in the spirit of Elijah, they were a "congregation" that insisted on searching the hills for their former "pastor"! The cloud had clearly moved, but they preferred things as they had been. They weren't happy about having a "new" prophet.

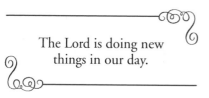

The Lord is doing new things in our day.

The Lord is doing new things in our day; some "unknowns" are speaking under the unction of the Holy Spirit. They have a message, but many will refuse to receive it from any but "prominent" ministers. They are just like the sons of the prophets.

These men shamed Elisha into sending them to look for Elijah. Elisha knew he was gone, but they would not be convinced. They had to find it out for themselves. Take heed from their example: If you realize you are refusing to follow the cloud, don't try to defend your position. God is the strength and saving defense to His anointed! (See Psalm 28:8.) He will have His way!

If you are on the receiving end of such resistance, don't become angry at those who reject you. And don't try to become God, controlling the situation and the people involved. Instead, simply love them and let them go.

It is important to respond correctly to rejection. An improper response can foster resentment, anger, and bitterness. Bitterness will not only defile you, but others as well (see Heb. 12:15).

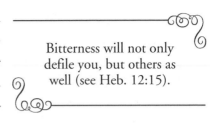

Bitterness will not only defile you, but others as well (see Heb. 12:15).

Completing God's Plan

The sons of the prophets searched for Elijah for three days (see 2 Kings 2:17). The number three is symbolic of completion and perfection. (Jesus was three days in the grave; Jonah was three nights in the belly of the whale.) The inner prompting in the sons of the prophets had to run its course.

And what did Elisha do during those three days? Did he grumble in resentment and bitterness? No. He calmly awaited their return in Jericho—which is the only way to overcome resentments, rejection, and bitterness. Jericho is the picture of ultimate victory through praise and worship. When negative feelings begin to disturb your mind and heart, go to Jericho for three days.

David declared: *"Bless the Lord, O my soul; and **all that is within me,** bless His holy name"* (Ps. 103:1). The word "all" in this verse includes the temptation to pity oneself, to feel rejected, and to become angry or bitter. Before we cross the Jordan, it is easy to cling to these feelings, but after crossing, we refuse to give place to them because we realize that they hinder God's Spirit in us.

Like Elisha, we need to come back to Jericho and remain until the work is done.

Over the years, many ministries have endured unjust criticism. Division has resulted. The Church must resist division and promote unity. Elisha demonstrates his commitment to God's purposes: Elijah was taken from him, the sons of the prophets rejected him, they misunderstood (and even stalled) God's plan; yet Elisha remained focused. He simply returned to Jericho and waited patiently (see 2 Kings 2:18).

We can and must do the same. Let's allow the words of the apostle Peter to guide our hearts today:

> *For this finds favor, if for the sake of conscience toward God a person bears up under sorrows when suffering unjustly. For what credit is there if, when you sin and are harshly treated, you endure it with patience? But if when you do what is right and suffer for it you patiently endure it, this finds favor with God. For you have been called for this purpose, since Christ also suffered for you, leaving you an example for you to follow in His steps, who committed no sin, nor was any deceit found in His mouth; and while being reviled, He did not revile in return; while suffering, He uttered no threats, but kept entrusting Himself to Him who judges righteously...* (1 Peter 2:19-23).

POINTS TO PONDER

1. "Although the sons of the prophets admitted that Elisha was operating in the spirit of Elijah, they were a 'congregation' that insisted on searching the hills for their former 'pastor'!"

   Do you often find yourself wishing for the "good ol' days"? Do you wistfully look back at past miracles and experiences you had with God while being discontent and dissatisfied with your current state? Do you believe that God has even greater things in store for your future?

2. Read First Peter 2:19-23 again, and then ask God to help you follow Christ's example.

CHAPTER 11

THE MENACE OF "MUDDY" WATERS

Then the men of the city said to Elisha, "Behold now, the situation of this city is pleasant, as my lord sees; but the water is bad and the land is unfruitful."
(2 Kings 2:19)

After the sons of the prophets returned from their three-day search for Elijah, the men of Jericho told Elisha of the challenges they faced in their "pleasant" city of Jericho.

Their assessment could well apply to the condition of the Charismatic Church today. The situation of the Church is pleasant enough, but the water is tainted and the spiritual ground is not yielding all that it should.

It seems like a contradiction, doesn't it? How can something be both pleasant and unfruitful? Many good things have occurred in the Charismatic Church: people have been saved, healed, and filled with the Spirit; many have been freed from the torments of the enemy. But God wants to take what He has given us and cause it to spread far and wide!

> Visitation from God does not accomplish all He intends if we fail to impact society at large.

The great revivals of the past have had a tremendous impact on the world. Visitation from God does not accomplish all He intends if we fail to impact society at large. Yet, the outward issues of people and societies are not our greatest concerns. What man really needs is a reconstruction of his inner nature. We want our laws and our people to reflect godly ideals; yet until hearts are transformed, the ways of sin will remain.

We have seen evidence of this truth in our own day. In spite of an emphasis on church growth and new methods of outreach, sin abounds and iniquity prevails. Fighting to change our laws may be helpful, but even the best laws cannot change the heart of man.

So, what is God asking of the Church today? Why aren't we functioning with the same power as the Church of the Book of Acts? Many boast about having "New Testament" churches, but where is this New Testament Church? I know many ministries in the land are attempting to build according to the apostolic pattern, but for the Church to function at the level it did in the first century, our methods must be purified.

It is time to return to ancient pathways and age-old foundations (see Isa. 58:12). We must build on the foundation of Christ and His principles. The Church is *the* covenant community. In the Old Testament, Zion was the picture of the glory of God resting with His people. Zion also speaks of the New Testament Church. Hebrews 12:22 declares that we, the Church, have come to Mount Zion. It is a picture of the Church in all her glory and power.

Many are crying out to God for a return to the pattern of the Book of Acts. The question is, *How do we get there?* We'll discover the answer in the next chapter as we study how Elisha purified the waters and restored the land of Jericho using a "new jar" and some salt (see 2 Kings 2:19-22).

For now, let's establish the importance of a new vessel and explore some of the impurities that have crept into the Church over the years.

Prepare a New Wineskin

The word *new* is significant in Scripture. The psalmist exhorts us to *"sing to the Lord a new song"* (Ps. 96:1). The word *new* here implies something fresh and alive. Paul reminds us that if *"anyone is in Christ, he is a **new** creature"* (2 Cor. 5:17). I can't help sensing in my spirit that God wants to do a new thing in the earth.

> If our eyes are on the former things that God has done, we will not be aware of the new things He desires to do.

Consider the prophecy recorded in Isaiah 43:18-19:

> *Do not call to mind the former things, or ponder things of the past. Behold, I will do something **new**, now it will spring forth; will you not be aware of it?*

If our eyes are on the former things that God has done, we will not be aware of the new things He desires to do. The outpourings that have occurred over the past century or so had their place and purpose; yet many who experienced those moves of God first-hand have opposed subsequent outpourings.

In the 1950s, the great healing revivalists came to the forefront of the Pentecostal movement. Several men and women rose to places of prominence and formed crusade-oriented ministries that took them around the globe. When their day was over, many of them could not accept the loss of fame and began using gimmickry to sustain their ministries.

These men and women had genuine callings from the Lord. But the intent of God has not been to focus on one man or one woman. God began to balance this aspect of the Charismatic movement in the late 1960s and early 1970s with an awareness of Body ministry, the equipping of the saints for the work of the ministry (see Eph. 4:12).

This awareness notwithstanding, the city can remain pleasant and unfruitful—in part because God needs to do something *new*. While Elisha asked for a new jar, Jesus called the Jews into something new (and how hard it was for the Pharisees and scribes to release their traditions for what Jesus offered). Yet Jesus made the case for transformation perfectly clear:

> *Nor do people put **new** wine into old wineskins; otherwise the wineskins burst, and the wine pours out, and the wineskins are ruined; but they put new wine into fresh wineskins, and both are preserved* (Matthew 9:17).

New wine needs a new wineskin. Why did the outpouring of the 1960s and 1970s not bring about a greater, more lasting impact? Because men sought to put the new wine into old wineskins such as outmoded traditions, denominationalism, and sectarian spirits that have hindered the Church for centuries.

We have tried to contain the move of God within a denominational setting. As a result, a sectarian spirit has produced barriers of elitism among established denominations and among some "independent" fellowships that are more denominational than they care to admit.

Some factions claim to have the "true concept" of local church autonomy; others claim to have "the" revelation of the fullness of the Spirit; still others claim to be the only ones who *worship the Father in spirit and truth"* (John 4:23). There is even a sect of Christendom that claims to have "the" revelation on church government. This group warns that failure to embrace their unique revelation will doom you to hell.

All these so-called revelations have produced a snobby, stuffy, self-centered, fleshly division into manmade parties or sects. These exclusive "clubs" are "old" news. Worse, they deny the Lord the joy of seeing us made one even as He and the Father are one (see John 17:11).

God loves His children whether they are in denominational or nondenominational churches. What God hates, is *denominationalism,* which is nothing less than the revived Babylonian spirit seeking to destroy the work of Christ. Denominationalism has kept the Body of Christ divided for centuries. As a result, the Bride is not ready for His return!

We seem to expect God to unify the Church; but He has called us to do it. If we wait for Him to "fix" the problem, we will wait forever. The job is ours to do; we are to be bridge-builders and barrier-busters. It is up to us to embrace the Body as a whole and as individuals. This is part of our being transformed into the image of Christ.

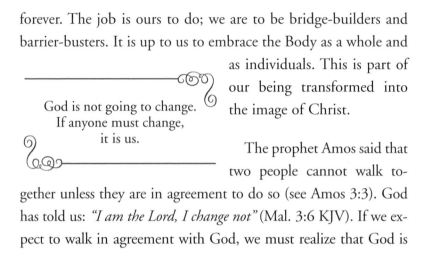

God is not going to change. If anyone must change, it is us.

The prophet Amos said that two people cannot walk together unless they are in agreement to do so (see Amos 3:3). God has told us: *"I am the Lord, I change not"* (Mal. 3:6 KJV). If we expect to walk in agreement with God, we must realize that God is not going to change. If anyone must change, it is us.

Division: An Old Enemy

The denominational spirit is nothing new. It existed in the early days of the Church. In Acts 1:8, as He was ascending to the throne, Jesus mandated His disciples to await the time when every enemy is made a footstool for His feet. He said very clearly:

> *…but you will receive power when the Holy Spirit has come upon you; and you shall be My witnesses both in Jerusalem, and in all Judea and Samaria, and even to the remotest part of the earth* (Acts 1:8 KJV).

Note the progression: Jerusalem, Judea, Samaria, and the farthest point on the globe.

When God birthed the Church in power, it was glorious. The Spirit of God came and fulfilled the Feast of Pentecost and thousands were ingathered. As a result, the Jerusalem Church grew to more than 8,000 within the first few months. Tremendous miracles, signs, and wonders accompanied the apostolic ministry. Unfortunately, the Jerusalem Church grew complacent.

The fault lay with the leadership. In Acts 10, Peter received a vision while on a rooftop in Joppa. This vision prompted him to repent. God wanted to bring the Gospel to the Gentiles, but Peter had drawn a dividing line; he saw himself as a Jew (and therefore "pure") and considered Gentiles to be unclean. However, Jesus' work on Calvary was for everyone who would receive it.

Because they were proud of their heritage, lineage, and callings, Peter and James became impediments to the Gospel. Imagine! Peter had

> Jesus' work on Calvary was for everyone who would receive it.

seen Jesus minister to the Roman centurion and heard the Master marvel at the faith of this Gentile (see Matt. 8:5-13). He also heard Jesus say that *"...many will come from east and west, and recline at the table with Abraham, Isaac and Jacob in the kingdom of heaven"* (Matt. 8:11).

Peter heard, but did not perceive. In John 4, Jesus reached out to the Samaritan woman. The Jews never interacted with Samaritans. Yet Peter saw revival brought to Samaria through that woman. Still, his heart remained hard. After all of that, he still had to be rebuked by God.

Peter finally "got it"—but not until eight or nine years *after* the Lord's ascension! That was when he went, in obedience to God's will, yet with great reservation, to Cornelius' home, where the entire household was saved and filled with the Holy Spirit.

The cautionary tale is this: After nine years, Church leadership had done nothing to extend the message beyond arbitrary, man-made "boundaries" and fulfill the mandate of Acts 1:8. They were content to stay in the confines of their own little revelation.

This explains why Stephen had to be the first martyr of the Church. Notice what happened in Acts 11:19:

> *So then those who were **scattered** because of the*
> *persecution that occurred in connection with Stephen*
> *made their way to Phoenicia and Cyprus and Antioch....*

Do you see the sovereign hand of God? The Church at Jerusalem had grown inward; it was sectarian and denominational. They refused to reach outward in times of peace, so God sent a time of persecution. The very enemies of the Gospel were the instrument God used to scatter the seed. Stephen's death led to widespread persecution, which in turn led to a scattering, or diaspora, of the believers.

God was tired of His children playing church; there was work to be done. Jesus had instructed His disciples to go to Jerusalem, Judea, Samaria, and the whole planet. Yet during the first eight or nine years, the Church had not reached beyond Judea. Within a matter of days after the stoning of Stephen and the scattering of the Church, Philip brought revival to Samaria, and others went to reach places like Phoenicia, Cyprus, and Antioch.

How crucial it is that we understand this: God will always see to it that His will is done. In Old Testament times, King Cyrus of Persia was considered an enemy of God's people. Yet in Isaiah he is called *"Cyrus His anointed"* (Isa. 45:1). Why? Because Cyrus was used of God. God will use whatever and whomever He chooses to bring His people out of the old and into the new.

Too often, churches used of God as centers of great revival are later whittled down to nothing. Is it possible that we have failed in some way to fully obey the purpose for which God raised up a mighty

> God will always see to it that His will is done....[He] will use whatever and whomever He chooses to bring His people out of the old and into the new.

work? Until the leadership takes responsibility for spiritual missteps and shortfalls and begins to exercise their delegated authority in a responsible and godly manner, these churches will struggle endlessly. With no progressive vision, the people will perish spiritually, as Solomon warned in Proverbs 29:18.

What Are We Reproducing?

We reproduce after our kind in the spiritual as well as the natural realms. In Acts 11:19, Luke tells us that, after the diaspora, some of the disciples who fled to Phoenicia, Cyprus, and Antioch were *"…speaking the word to **no one except to Jews alone.**"*

Somehow these disciples of the apostles at Jerusalem got the impression that the Gospel was only for the Jews. Peter and James had reproduced the sectarian spirit in their disciples! Who were Paul's biggest troublemakers? They were called *Judaizers*. They were part of the original sect of the Church at Jerusalem; they preached circumcision and observance of the Mosaic Law as essential to salvation in Christ. Every place Paul carried the Gospel, the Judaizers followed close behind to leaven the lump with their heresy.

Paul told the church at Galatia that Peter's sectarian spirit, as well as that of James's disciples, was hypocrisy and a stumbling block. Paul maintained that any Gospel other than his Gospel was false, and that those who preached such alternative views were accursed (see Gal. 1:8).

We are not saying that Peter was preaching a false Gospel, but his failure to make a clean break with Judaism led to a legalistic spirit that worsened in the next generation of believers. What was allowed by the Jerusalem apostles in moderation produced an excess in their disciples.

However, Luke revealed some positive news in Acts 11:20: *"But there were some of them, men of Cyprus and Cyrene, who came to Antioch and began speaking to the Greeks also, preaching the Lord Jesus."*

God still had a group of people obedient to the original intent of the message, and as a result the Church at Antioch was birthed. The Antioch church became the very platform from which the program of God was to be launched to evangelize the world.

Let's study their powerful example next.

POINTS TO PONDER

1. "How can something be both pleasant and unfruitful?"
   Consider the churches in your area. Are some of them
   pleasant yet unfruitful?

   Consider your own life. Is it pleasant but relatively
   unfruitful?

2. "We reproduce after our kind in the spiritual as well as the
   natural realms." What kind of spiritual children are you
   reproducing and bringing into the family of God?

CHAPTER 12

THE CLEAR STREAM AT ANTIOCH

*He said, "Bring me a new jar, and put salt in it." So
they brought it to him. He went out to the spring of
water and threw salt in it and said, "Thus says the Lord,
'I have purified these waters; there shall not be from
there death or unfruitfulness any longer.'" So the waters
have been purified to this day, according to the word of
Elisha which he spoke.*
(2 Kings 2:20-22)

God wants to do a new thing in the earth today. The dynamics of change are much as they were 2,000 years ago: God-initiated change reveals the human tendency to fall into pseudo-religious traps and fleshly ways of doing things. We get so comfortable with programs, plans, and accomplishments that when new directions emerge, we are reluctant to change.

The farther we stray from God's direction, the more resistant we become to the idea of change. Instead of

> The farther we stray from God's direction, the more resistant we become to the idea of change.

finding our security in Him and trusting Him to lead us forward to *wherever* He wants us to go, we shrink back from shifts that threaten our control. Little by little, we become territorial, each of us guarding "our" piece of turf.

The result? Disunity. It may seem insignificant at first, but it is anathema to the Body of Christ.

Unity and Purity in Covenant

The "new thing" God wants to do requires us to become new wineskins, vessels ready and able to contain God's new vintage! It will also require us to value and promote the overall health of the Body of Christ. The best health insurance for the Church is one of the world's oldest curing agents: salt.

In Second Kings 2:20, Elisha asked for salt to be placed in a new jar. Numbers 18:19 speaks of a "*covenant of salt.*" A covenant of salt was irrevocable and binding.

The New Testament Church is a community of believers related one to another through covenant. In this hour, we must be bound together by strong cords. We must not be quick to run from problems, relationships, or confrontations. The Body needs to come together by a covenant of salt.

In Leviticus 2:13, we see that salt was required by God in the offerings of the Temple. In ancient times its value was equal to gold. In the Eastern world, salt has been used to ratify agreements. "Salt stands for permanence and incorruption."[1] It is a symbol of fidelity, commitment, and constancy. To God's people, a covenant of salt was a reminder of the faithfulness required in the keeping of covenant. Jesus said: *"Salt is good; but if the salt becomes unsalty, with what will you make it salty again? Have salt in yourselves, and be at peace with one another"* (Mark 9:50).

Jesus reminded His disciples that they were (as we are) *"the salt of the earth"* (Matt. 5:13). It was the salt that Elisha put in the new jar that caused the waters to be purified. Salt speaks of the Church, the covenant community in action. It speaks of loyalty and fidelity to Christ and each other.

Too often, we have seen halfhearted commitment to unity in the local church. When things don't go our way, we pack our belongings and drag our frustrations to another fellowship. As a result, we never grow up. We enter new situations, but we remain unchanged. As long as our issues go unchallenged, the roots of our problems will cause the same bad fruit to sprout up over and over again.

> As long as our issues go unchallenged, the roots of our problems will cause the same bad fruit to sprout up over and over again.

We need to allow God to purge us. We must recognize our issues and our need for change. Pointing a finger at the other guy and praying for God to change him skirts the issue and keeps us in bondage. The truth is that God wants to change *us* (which is easier said than done).

He wants unity, but unity comes at a price—it will cost us the right to have things our way all the time. Unity requires maturity; becoming a unified church is a process of purification. That purification comes by fire. God will turn up the heat in order for the gold (His people) to be purified. The heat is uncomfortable, but it is the only way to bring impurities to the surface and eliminate them.

Unity comes at a price—it will cost us the right to have things our way all the time.

According to Isaiah 4:4, God purges Zion by *"the spirit of judgment and the spirit of burning."* If it gets hot where you are, there's probably a reason for it. If you are loyal to God, you'll endure the heat. If you are loyal to the Body and understand covenant commitment, you won't search out another church because you'll realize that God is turning up the fire there as well!

Salt will not dissolve in the presence of intense heat; it can withstand extreme temperatures. The basis for unity is salt: loyalty and fidelity. Paul implored the church at Ephesus to be *"diligent to preserve the unity of the Spirit in the bond of peace"* (Eph. 4:3). The word *preserve* means "to watch over" or "keep guard"; the word diligent means an "aggressive earnestness and zeal." "Have salt," said Jesus, "and be at peace with one another."

Why is unity so important? Remember that, when Elisha was at Jericho, the water had to be purified first. Then the land reaped the blessing (see 2 Kings 2:21). So it is in the Kingdom of God. Listen to Jesus' words as He prayed for the Church:

> *That they may all be **one**; even as You, Father, are in Me and I in You, that they also may be in Us, so that **the world may believe** that You sent Me* (John 17:21).

Salt leads to purification; loyalty and fidelity lead to unity. Unity leads to a release of the Spirit of God to those outside the

Kingdom. Through our expression of oneness, the glory of the risen Christ is revealed and many will believe.

Through our expression of oneness, the glory of the risen Christ is revealed and many will believe.

The Antioch Message

We have seen resistance to the moves of God as demonstrated by the sons of the prophets in Elisha's day and by the elitism of the first-century Church. Yet, those who resist God are only one side of the story.

This was certainly true in first-century Antioch, where God found a willing remnant among the Greeks. The church there serves as a model for what God wants to accomplish in every local church.

To benefit from their example, we need to discover the source of Antioch's strength. The Antioch church sprang from the diaspora. When believers were scattered by persecution, they preached to the Greeks in Antioch. They didn't exclude anyone from the hope of salvation; they simply shared the Gospel.

Their message was the source of their strength and remains the very foundation of New Covenant faith: it is message of *the lordship of Jesus Christ*. The right message birthed the church at Antioch and kept it in synch with God's plans.

This message of Jesus' lordship is the only fitting foundation. Christ was exalted following His death and resurrection expressly *to be Lord!* Therefore, the Church must adhere to this message.

> Christ was exalted following His death and resurrection expressly *to be Lord!*

It's the only one that will endure the shaking that is already upon us and is sure to increase in the days ahead.

Obedience and submission to Christ are essential. When Jesus turned the water into wine at the wedding in Cana, Mary told the servants: *"Whatever He says to you, do it"* (John 2:5). The Church needs to come to this place of being obedient to Christ in all He requires. This obedience must exist in both the pulpit and the pews.

Servants as Leaders

The church at Antioch wasn't built around big personalities; it was built on the Christ of glory. In Revelation 21:23 we find that the only light in the City of God is the light of the Lamb. There is no natural light in the Holiest of All, only the light of God's glory. No flesh will glory in His presence. God is stripping and shaking us so that only the light of His glory remains!

The ordinary believers at Antioch took personal responsibility for evangelizing the lost. God hasn't called the big names to win the lost; in fact, if we read Ephesians 4:11-13 in context, we find that the purpose of the evangelist is to *teach the sheep* to evangelize. Sheep reproduce sheep.

After the Antioch church was formed, the Jerusalem church commissioned Barnabas to oversee it. Barnabas was not an opportunist; he sought the riches of Christ rather than his own gain.

He was free of the legalistic spirit that was so pervasive in the church in Jerusalem; therefore, he was free to be productive in his calling.

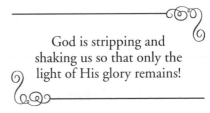

God is stripping and shaking us so that only the light of His glory remains!

Barnabas's name tells us a lot about him; it means "encourager." As an apostolic minister (see Eph. 4:11), Barnabas came to help set the house of God at Antioch in order. Notice how he accomplished this:

> *When he arrived and witnessed the grace of God, he rejoiced and began to encourage them all with resolute heart to remain true to the Lord...* (Acts 11:23).

Three keys reveal why Barnabas was so well received and effective. Scripture says he:

1. *Witnessed the grace of God.* Barnabas saw that God was alive and well in the church; he recognized God's tangible grace manifested in the believers at Antioch.

2. *Rejoiced.* Barnabas shared in their joy and joined in the excitement at Antioch. (Is a pattern beginning to emerge in your thinking?)

3. Encouraged them all. Barnabas's verbal ministry was one of encouragement. He didn't quench the people's zeal by saying, "Stop evangelizing until we mature the lambs." The only demand he placed upon the people was obedience to God (*"...remain true to the Lord"*).

Luke went on to say that Barnabas had an effective ministry because *"...he was a good man, and full of the Holy Spirit and of faith. And considerable numbers were brought to the Lord"* (Acts 11:24).

Barnabas: A Team Player

A mighty move of God was already underway when Barnabas arrived; but he encouraged an explosion! Yet, at the height of the activity, *"*[Barnabas] *left for Tarsus to look for Saul..."* (Acts 11:25).

What possessed Barnabas to leave at a time like that? Barnabas realized he could not lead the church alone. He was humble enough to acknowledge that he didn't have all the gifts needed to shepherd the flock.

Many fine leaders have crashed and burned trying to do the job alone. The result is disastrous; the Body can only be fully nourished when *"every joint supplies"* its God-ordained contribution to the mission (Eph. 4:16).

The "lone ranger" minister also lacks the maturity that comes from being sharpened by co-laborers. Eventually, the sheep realize the imbalance and begin to despise their leader's authority. In time, they will scatter, further weakening the church.

How desperately the Body needs team ministry! Team members play for the benefit of the organization. The result is a healthy community. But if one member hogs the ball, the rest of the team loses heart. When team members are stifled by the insecurity of a senior leader, the seeds of rebellion are sown and the Body is fragmented.

Barnabas demonstrated that we *need each other*. His departure revealed his confidence in the Antioch team. Barnabas had raised up capable

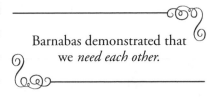

Barnabas demonstrated that we *need each other*.

leaders during his time there, and he trusted them. We don't know exactly how long he was away from Antioch, but since Luke implies that Barnabas had to search for Paul, we can assume that it was some time before he found him.

Once Barnabas brought Saul back to Antioch, the two men taught as a team for a full year (see Acts 11:25-26).

The Saul Story

Barnabas hadn't seen Saul for a decade or more. Saul, a former persecutor of the Church (he supported the stoning of Stephen), experienced a dramatic conversion on the Damascus road and was mightily called to preach the Gospel before kings and princes.

Saul received a great revelation and found himself making tents in the wilderness at Tarsus for 14 years! The apostle endured many hardships, including five separate floggings of 39 lashes apiece (see 2 Cor. 11:24-27).

Much of the persecution that Saul (also known as *Paul,* according to Acts 13:9) endured took place at the hands of Jews. He had returned to his hometown proclaiming Jesus; the rabbis called him a blasphemer and ordered him scourged (nearly to death). According to tradition, Saul's wife deserted him as a result of his newfound faith.

For Saul, Judaism was lacking. All that seemed to remain was the bitter fruit of legalism, the very spirit God had rooted out from Saul's own heart. Saul recognized its awful power to blind the Jews. More and more, he also recognized the power of the Gospel to save them.

In his wilderness time, God made known to Saul His full intent and revealed the plan for His glorious Church and the New Jerusalem. Over the course of 14 years in Tarsus, the pattern for the true Zion of God was birthed; the revelation would be fully revealed and received in God's perfect timing.

Meanwhile, God had begun to shift the Church's center from Jerusalem to Antioch. This allowed Him to prepare a new people (the Gentiles) who were untouched by tradition and open to the new things He was doing. Hence, when the time was ripe, God sent Barnabas to bring Saul to the forefront of this new move. The timing was quintessentially God: Antioch was ready for Saul and Saul was ready for Antioch.

What happened in Antioch could not have happened 14 years earlier in Jerusalem; the people of God simply weren't ready for it.

A People Prepared by God

Today, God is preparing a people who haven't been molded by the traditions of past visitations. They are simply hungry for truth. He is grooming ministries in a "wilderness of Tarsus," where every ounce of legalism is being driven out and an understanding of Christ and His finished work is being imparted. The greatest revelation of God's glory is yet to be seen!

> God is preparing a people who haven't been molded by the traditions of past visitations. They are simply hungry for truth.

At Antioch, Saul and Barnabas taught for an entire year, and revival continued. Antioch is where disciples of Christ were first called *Christians* (see Acts 11:26). There was something so radically new about this visitation that believers inherited a new name. Before that, God's people went only by the name of Jews.

Now, God had brought Jew and Gentile together under a single banner. In Isaiah 62:2 the prophet, speaking of God's chosen people, said: *"...You will be called by a new name, which the mouth of the Lord will designate."* At Antioch, the *"chosen generation"* mentioned in First Peter 2:9 (KJV) had a new name that pointed to their Head.

A Christian is one who is "like Christ." There was something identifiable about this company of believers at Antioch. It caused the citizens there to recognize their resemblance to Him. The Church, the house of God, reflected the character of its Builder!

Endnote

1. James M. Freeman and Harold Chadwick, *The New Manners and Customs of the Bible* (Orlando, FL: Bridge-Logos, 1998), 143.

POINTS TO PONDER

1. "As long as our issues go unchallenged, the roots of our problems will cause the same bad fruit to sprout up over and over again." Examine your church, family, and even yourself. Are there issues that seem to be recurring problems? Ask God to help you discover the roots of these issues and teach you how to prevent them from coming back again.

2. "If we read Ephesians 4:11-13 in context, we find that the purpose of the evangelist is to *teach the sheep* to evangelize. Sheep reproduce sheep." Are you answering the call to evangelize? Are you being fruitful and multiplying?

CHAPTER 13

JORDAN AND BEYOND

There is more we can learn from Antioch. They were a worshiping church and a body that availed itself of the richness of the fivefold ministry.

> *He gave some as apostles, and some as prophets,* and some as evangelists, and some as pastors and teachers, for the equipping of the saints for the work of service, to the building up of the body of Christ; until we all attain to the unity of the faith, and of the knowledge of the Son of God, to a mature man, to the measure of the stature which belongs to the fullness of Christ (Ephesians 4:11-13).

Apostles and prophets are part of Christ's provision for the Church. God still has prophets who declare a holy and righteous standard and move in the realm of revelation with a word of knowledge to reveal past, present, and future events. God

> Apostles and prophets are part of Christ's provision for the Church.

said He would not do anything without first revealing it to His prophets (see Amos 3:7).

Yet, many fear prophetic ministry. This is partly due to abuses of the prophetic office. However, there is danger in throwing out the good with the bad. That danger must have been evident in the early Church. Paul cautioned believers at Thessalonica, saying: *"**Do not despise** prophetic utterances. But examine everything carefully; **hold fast** to that which is good"* (1 Thess. 5:20-21).

This is God's balance. There are many in ministry who embrace the truths of the fivefold ministry and the gifts of the Spirit, yet forbid them to operate. They say their restrictions can be supported scripturally; but I suspect they are rooted in a negative bias regarding the gifts.

We need to allow prophetic ministry to bring the Word of God to the Body, and we need to obey the Word when it comes! If we do not obey, we will pay the price. The questions will invariably arise: *What if a false prophet arises? Will the Church blindly follow the next Jim Jones and commit mass suicide at his word?*

The truth is, there have always been and always will be those who lead others astray. But when mature ministries are functioning together in the pattern of Ephesians 4:11 and keeping each other balanced in covenant relationship, we will see a healthy functioning of the prophetic ministry in the midst of God's people.

Trust the Integrity of God's Word

These are decision-making days. Deep theological debates are not the solution; what is needed is agreement on a simple issue of faith—the integrity of the Word of God. God says He gave us apostles and prophets. More and more, we are beginning to see them in the Body of Christ, but many still resist these representatives of the fivefold ministry, while claiming to embrace the mandate of Ephesians 4:11.

Apostles and prophets are functioning and blessing the Body where they are recognized, received, and allowed to minister. Acts 13 points out that there is no room in the New Covenant Church for a one-man show. God's order for the Church is *plurality with one chief among equals.* I have an anointing in one area of ministry; you have an anointing in another. It would be foolish and presumptuous of me to tell you how to function in your anointing.

> Apostles and prophets are functioning and blessing the Body where they are recognized, received, and allowed to minister.

In Antioch, a diverse group of prophets and teachers functioned together as a team: Barnabas was originally from Jerusalem. Simeon is widely believed to have been an African man who carried the cross of Christ up the Via Dolorosa (see Luke 23:26). Lucius was also of Cyrene. Manaen had been brought up with King Herod (see Acts 13:1). Saul hailed from Tarsus.

Antioch was a metropolitan city, an ancient melting pot. The eldership represented every strata of society. In God's house all were equal. A Roman soldier singled out a black man to carry an ignominious cross upon which the Savior would be crucified (prejudice ran rampant even then). But in the house of God, Simeon was exalted to a place of leadership over the Father's affairs!

Manaen, though quite wealthy according to historians, shared equality with others and ministered in the house of the Lord. Each man had a unique ministry. Their various backgrounds, nationalities, and occupations shaped the effectiveness of the church in Antioch.

Worship and the New Wine

Another characteristic of the church at Antioch was that they ministered to the Lord (see Acts 13:2). In other words, they were worshipers! We too are called to worship God—from Gilgal...to Bethel...to Jericho, Jordan, and beyond.

God is seeking worshipers in this hour! We need to learn how to minister to the Lord. *Minister* was a word used by the Greeks to describe service to the city or state that exceeded what we might see as normal obligations. A Greek citizen was expected to do more than hold a job and pay taxes; he was required to donate his services to the body politic. This service was called *ministry*. (Jury duty and volunteer work would be comparable activities in our society.)

All that we do with Christ at the center is worship to God. Not only our singing and our praises; not only our dancing and our giving and serving; but everything we do in our daily lives that acknowledges Him, both in church and everywhere we go, is called *worship*.

The writer to the Hebrews put it this way:

> *Through **Him** then [all acceptable worship is through Christ by the power of the Spirit], let us **continually***

offer up a sacrifice of praise to God, that is, the fruit of lips that give thanks to His name (Hebrews 13:15).

God is looking for a Church committed to worship. Some have made a ritual of worship; they worship the act of worship! God wants us to worship *Him!* We are living in a day when God wants to purify us and the worship we offer, because true worship releases the new wine.

> God is looking for a Church committed to worship.

Fasting, Prayer, Prophecy, and Fruit

Luke, the writer of Acts, also revealed that the eldership and the body at Antioch fasted and prayed. We need to have seasons of fasting and prayer in the Church. It was during such a season of fasting and prayer that critical direction came to the church at Antioch.

> *While they were ministering to the Lord and fasting, the Holy Spirit said, "Set apart for Me Barnabas and Saul for the work to which I have called them"* (Acts 13:2).

How did the Holy Spirit communicate what He said? Through the *prophets!* Prophetic ministry yielded to God, pointed the direction, and said, "This is the way, walk in it" (see Isa. 30:21). An atmosphere of worship and prayer will bring the prophetic anointing to a people committed to covenant relationship in the house of God.

Through the prophetic anointing, the Lord revealed His plans for Saul and Barnabas. It became clear that the word of the Lord that came to Antioch through these men was not just for Antioch. It was to be sown elsewhere as well. Therefore, God called for the men to be set apart and sent out from Antioch.

God has been stirring the Body of Christ to plant new works around the world in our day, too. An understanding of the apostolic is growing in local churches today. With it comes the realization that churches can reproduce churches.

In response to the word of the Lord, the church at Antioch reproduced itself. That is an act of worship! Unlike the Jerusalem apostles, these men went all over the world with their message. When some believers chose to withhold the Gospel from certain groups, churches like the one at Antioch were released to reach them. The same is true today; if certain churches will not embrace what God is doing, He will release the fivefold ministry elsewhere.

> If certain churches will not embrace what God is doing, He will release the fivefold ministry elsewhere.

Saul and Barnabas were sent out by the laying on of hands; they were commissioned not merely by the Spirit, but also with the witness and blessing of the local church. Notice also that no ministry was sent out alone. Saul and Barnabas were a team. Many traveling ministries today would be more fruitful if they were plugged into a local church and functioned as part of a team effort. I believe deeply that the face of itinerant ministry will change radically in the days ahead as the Church comes to grips with its true purpose.

If such ministry is to survive in the coming days, those involved will have to reprioritize and reevaluate their purposes to ensure that they are fulfilling the mandate of Ephesians 4:11-12. The Church needs to realize that most souls who need to be saved aren't going to be in the meetings; they're going to be out on the streets.

> The Church needs to realize that most souls who need to be saved aren't going to be in the meetings; they're going to be out on the streets.

To reach them, we will need to leave the place of conversion (Gilgal)...reach outside of God's house (Bethel)...beyond the valley of Jericho where the Church's battles are waged and won...all the way to Jordan where the effectiveness of the cross is seen not only in us, but *through* us as others pass through the waters of death and into the life of Christ. And once there, we must be prepared to go anyplace else that God will take us.

Transition and even greater glory are ahead.

POINTS TO PONDER

1. What were some of the characteristics of the church in Antioch?

2. "The Church needs to realize that most souls who need to be saved aren't going to be in the meetings; they're going to be out on the streets." Ask yourself: *Am I willing to go wherever God wants me to go…even outside my comfort zone…in order to share His love with those who are lost?*

Chapter 14

The Elisha Season

As they were burying a man, behold, they saw a marauding band; and they cast the man into the grave of Elisha. And when the man touched the bones of Elisha he revived and stood up on his feet.

(2 Kings 13:21)

Everything that transpired between Elijah and Elisha on the path of synchronicity was perfectly orchestrated to produce the future God had already planned. Elisha clearly understood what his mentor offered. He recognized him as the unquestioned bearer of the anointing, the man who upheld God's cause in the midst of corruption and idolatry. He knew that Elijah had slain false prophets and raised the dead. Elisha wanted that anointing…and more.

Consider this miracle account from Elijah's ministry:

He stretched himself upon the child three times, and called to the Lord and said, "O Lord my God, I pray You, let this child's life return to him." The Lord heard the voice of Elijah, and the life of the child returned to him and he revived (1 Kings 17:21-22).

Elijah *"stretched himself upon"* a dead child, and God revived the boy. Furthermore, after both prophets were gone from the earth, a dead man was *"cast...into the grave of Elisha"* (2 Kings 13:21) and was revived when his body merely touched the dead prophet's bones!

Elisha's request for the double portion had not been a whim; it was God-inspired...and God-fulfilled. Increase is God's way. He wanted Elisha to learn from his mentor and surpass him. God foresaw the day that Elisha would raise the dead from his own grave!

The Ever-Advancing Kingdom

The Church has witnessed countless miracles over the centuries, many of them in our own lifetimes. Yet, God is not finished—not nearly. He is ready to pour out something greater than we have ever seen or dared to imagine.

That is why He is drawing us onto the path of synchronicity. He is drawing us to the place where divine connections are made and meaningful coincidences await our entrance onto the scene. The invisible realm is about to be revealed in our sight; but like Elisha, we must hunger for it.

The invisible realm is about to be revealed in our sight; but like Elisha, we must hunger for it.

Instead of "minding the shop" (*i.e.,* manning the pews) as the sons of the prophets did, we need to be out in the fields. It is time to dig into the soil of the next move of God, get our hands dirty, and prepare ourselves to receive the double portion God is so willing to bequeath.

Elisha allowed himself to be thrust onto the front lines. He saw and understood the hallmarks of Elijah's ministry. He perceived the significance of the mantle his master carried. The miracles spoke to Elisha; they pointed to the power of God operating through a willing vessel. The supernatural—including the chariots of fire and whirlwind that whisked away his master—served to alert Elisha to the ways in which God was moving.

Elisha read the signs correctly. He did not withdraw, but continued to advance. Instead of assuming that the season of miracles had peaked and the previous generation had seen all there was to see of the supernatural, Elisha operated in the belief that God was still moving, and in even greater ways than before. He remained positioned to participate; therefore, he became a conduit by which God could reach the next generation in powerful ways befitting their needs and their day.

Now is not the time to withdraw. Now is the time for us to carry the message of God's Kingdom forward.

Elisha's approach should be ours. Now is not the time to withdraw. Now is the time for us to carry the message of God's Kingdom forward, even as natural kingdoms and demonic realms are arrayed against us. Elijah and Elisha faced the same challenges; every generation does. They learned, as we must, that religious forms and traditions will not do. Only God's miracle-working power and grace will accomplish His plans and speak to those whose hearts are hardened through the deceptions and oppression of the enemy.

Embrace the season of the double portion. Continue to be a willing participant in the move of God. The time to decide is now. He longs for us to move with Him—but with or without us, God *will* advance His Kingdom.

Why Signs and Wonders?

Do you remember what Elisha did immediately after he retrieved the mantle that had fallen from the departing Elijah's shoulders?

Elisha walked to the banks of Jordan and struck the waters with the mantle that was now his to carry. The waters parted, just as they had for Elijah (see 2 Kings 2:13-14). Elisha wasted no time; he continued to move in the miraculous as his predecessor had done. He wasn't seeking the spotlight or trying to assert himself. He simply understood God's purposes. God had transferred the anointing because there was work to be done and a world to be reached.

Signs and wonders are equally important today; they accomplish very specific purposes in keeping with God's plan of salvation for lost people and nations. These are not displays of the spectacular designed to entertain. God is not into flash and glam; the sensational was never intended to substitute for the truly supernatural.

Nor will the sensational bring the power of God on the scene. Glory is the only atmosphere in which God will move. His miracle dynamics are not conjured by men and women, but supernaturally ignited by the Holy Spirit to achieve His ends. (The Father is not interested in creating fans, but genuine followers.)

> The Father is not interested in creating fans, but genuine followers.

God uses signs and wonders to affect the natural world in at least five key ways:

1. *Signs and wonders sustain God's cause against His enemies.* Signs and wonders not only relieve people of the enemy's oppression; they also push back the kingdom of darkness and facilitate the advancement of God's eternal plan.

2. *Signs and wonders exalt the faithful in the presence of God's enemies.* By investing His power in people, God draws clear battle lines between the "sheep" and the "goats" (see Matt. 25:33) and draws sharp distinctions between the intent of His followers and that of His enemies.

3. *Signs and wonders lead to the glorification of the Body of Christ.* Miracles, signs, and wonders highlight the reality and supernatural function of the Church. Those who are blinded to the living Christ or critical of His Body must reckon with both as they witness His miracles.

4. *Signs and wonders confuse the work of the enemy.* God's miracles undo the works of evil and stymie the forward motion of the enemy. These supernatural displays foster dissent and fear (and, therefore, confusion) in enemy ranks.

5. *Signs and wonders dismay those who oppose the move of God.* For those who feel it is their mission to resist God and His move, signs and wonders are strong reminders that their cause is futile. No power can overcome His power!

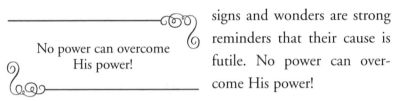
No power can overcome His power!

In every generation, signs and wonders serve to glorify the King of kings and expand His Kingdom.

Entrusting the Legacy

As He did in Elijah's day, God desires to entrust a legacy into the hands of His people. This transaction won't happen at Gilgal, Bethel, or Jericho. No! Jordan is the place where the transfer will occur.

The trek to Jordan isn't easy. Spiritual advancement is always accompanied by a battle. Like Elisha, we must peer into the invisible realm, plant our feet firmly in what we believe, and refuse to retreat. We must position ourselves to receive the mantle, even at the height of the struggle.

Part of this positioning has to do with preparation. Much of our preparation comes in the form of mentorship. Elijah successfully mentored Elisha. It was a hands-on endeavor rooted in a quality, purposeful relationship through which knowledge and insight were imparted *before* the mantle changed hands.

Elisha knew that if he wished to move in the power of God, he would have to connect deeply with someone who carried the anointing he desired. Their relationship was not accidental or incidental; it was meaningful.

Both men recognized the divine disposition of their relationship and their mutual need, one for the other. Elijah knew that Elisha was God's handpicked successor. Elisha knew that Elijah was God's proven vessel and the only one who had what Elisha needed.

Therefore, Elisha submitted himself to his mentor and fully engaged the process of preparation. At the same time, Elijah devoted himself to Elisha's development. His submission ensured Elisha's equipping and the continuation of the anointing.

The two men shared an affinity for the things of God. This affinity facilitated their mutual commitment. The result of their mutual commitment was effective learning. Therefore, their quality relationship made way for the spiritual exchange God had ordained.

Quality relationships lead to effective learning, and effective learning leads to improved performance. Whether in the corporate world or the spiritual realm, effectiveness is valued. Therefore, mentorship is prized by those who are committed to fulfilling their destinies.

Mentorship is not a one-way street; it is a two-sided dynamic: We are both mentored and called to mentor others. In this way, we will

> Quality relationships lead to effective learning, and effective learning leads to improved performance.

> Mentorship is not a one-way street; it is a two-sided dynamic: We are both mentored and called to mentor others.

continue to reproduce after our own kind. We will mentor and be mentored in the Holy Spirit to become a mighty people.

As a result there will be, in every generation, Elishas who come to carry forward the identifiable, genuine anointing of the Elijahs who went before them.

Gearing Up Until...*Suddenly*

How long did Elisha work in his father's fields before Elijah found him? How many times did Elisha groom his master's mantle before it fell from the sky and became his?

How long have you followed after God and sensed that *something* was coming? Are you among those whose anticipation is building right now? Or has your fervency been dampened through difficult seasons of opposition, setbacks, and disappointment?

Wherever you are in your walk with God, you are being tested as Elisha was. God is taking you beyond Elijah's ministry of hearing by the Word to Elisha's ministry of seeing by the Word—but you must keep your eyes fixed on Christ. If you do, you will see into the realms of God—the place where His moving begins.

The Father will change your perception of reality by revealing the storehouse of His glory, which is the realm of our inheritance in Him. He will cause you to move in that world and lay hold of its provision. He will show you all that He has stored up for His people. And He will anoint you to place in their hands exactly what they need—whether forgiveness, redemption, healing, restoration, miracles, faith, grace, or any other aspect of His salvation.

Just like Elisha, who sowed day after day in hopes of reaping the fruit for which he longed, we will need to remain vigilant and committed. It will be with us as it was with him: We will follow God from place to place, serving Him faithfully and wondering when the transfer of the anointing will occur. Then *suddenly!*—possibly in mid-sentence—the hand-off will be complete. As Elisha marveled at the chariots of fire descending into the natural realm, we will be awed as our long-awaited defining moment descends into plain view.

Remain in position. Your "suddenly" is on the way!

The Jordan Transfer

The Church is on the precipice of a new 500-year cycle. The double-portion anointing is about to be transferred from the Anointed Christ (whom Elijah foreshadowed) to His people (as typified by Elisha, our example of transition to resurrection power and greater works).

We are living in days of resurrection and restoration! God is grooming a people equipped with the Word and ready to move in signs, wonders, and miracles. At the same time, a cry for the genuine is rising up from one end of the earth

> God is grooming a people equipped with the Word and ready to move in signs, wonders, and miracles.

to the other. A new generation that longs for the authentic is coming onto the scene.

Like Elisha, they will not settle for mediocrity, substitutes, or forms of religion. They are looking to their spiritual forebears for an example. They want to see a company of believers who have paid the price to walk with the Anointed One. They know they must learn from those who have gone before them. At the same time, those to whom they look understand that the next generation is vital to the unfolding of this Elisha season.

God is preparing us for a great outpouring—a far more expansive reformation of society than we have ever known or read about. It is a season in which the army of God must be thoroughly furnished to complete the good works God is directing it to undertake.

Each "soldier" must be truth-ready, able to understand the marching orders and determined to move in the supernatural power of God. Why? To answer the cries of the millions and even billions of people worldwide who hunger for what they have not yet seen or heard. They are the ones who long to stand face to face with a miracle-working God who promises deliverance and then delivers people and nations before their very eyes.

Every soldier must also be ready to mentor someone in the up-and-coming generation who is ready to be "found." These are the modern-day Elishas who are in the field awaiting that someone whose assignment it is to prepare them for the hand-off of the anointing. They are seeking the "elders" who will show them how to reach into the invisible realm and carry out, by the anointing, the fullness of God's plan and provision for His world.

As we move together on God's path of synchronicity, we will witness the transfer of the anointing that removes the curse and breaks every yoke—the anointing of Christ that brings the reality of resurrection power to bear on every form of evil and every manifestation of the curse (see Deut. 27). But we must be willing to leave Gilgal, Bethel, and Jericho to head for Jordan.

Jordan is the pivot point for which God and His people yearn. Press forward to meet your destiny there. Watch the mantle fall from the sky. Pick it up; strike the waters of fear and satanic strongholds. See the God of Elijah move on your behalf to make a way where there was no way.

This is our Elisha season!

POINTS TO PONDER

1. "The invisible realm is about to be revealed in our sight; but like Elisha, we must hunger for it." Do you hunger to see the unseen? Or do you find yourself fearful of the unknown and thus satisfied with the status quo?

2. List five of the ways that God uses signs and wonders to affect the natural world.

3. "Mentorship is not a one-way street; it is a two-sided dynamic: we are both mentored and called to mentor others." Are you mentoring and/or being mentored? Why or why not?

4. Are you ready to pick up the mantle?

Author Ministry Page

For more information about Mark Chironna, please visit:
www.markchironna.com

Additional copies of this book and other
book titles from DESTINY IMAGE are
available at your local bookstore.

Call toll-free: 1-800-722-6774.

Send a request for a catalog to:

Destiny Image® Publishers, Inc.

P.O. Box 310
Shippensburg, PA 17257-0310

*"Speaking to the Purposes of God for This
Generation and for the Generations to Come."*

**For a complete list of our titles,
visit us at www.destinyimage.com.**